Ready, Steady, Go to School!

A Fun-Filled Guide for Parents to Prepare Their Children for Elementary School

By C. A. Callum

O'Brien Associates Group Publishing

direct or indirect, that are incurred as a result of the use of the information contained within this document, including, but not limited to, errors, omissions, or inaccuracies.

Table of Contents

Introduction

The goal of teaching a child is not to increase the amount of knowledge but to create possibilities for a child to invent and discover. —Jean Piaget, a Swiss Psychologist

Parenthood is indeed a beautiful blessing in life. Along with the pleasure of cherishing our children, we are endowed with a set of responsibilities to nurture and guide our children to be their best. As soon as the child is born, knowingly or unknowingly, we get involved in the process of teaching and training them. Whether it be the act of teaching them to smile or respond in their infancy, helping them take their first little steps in toddlerhood, or putting the initial few words in their mouth to speak, it all lies on the strong shoulders of a parent. As the little child grows, parents gear up to get started with a new and innovative phase of their child's life, which is elementary schooling. Often, in the excitement and rush to enroll the child in their first school, parents tend to skip a major milestone in their child's life—the preparatory phase or the training phase. However, many parents overlook what they are depriving their child of by doing so.

This process of training and preparing the child before elementary schooling is the very first important step toward learning in their life, as it introduces them to all the necessary survival skills like eating on their own, taking care of themselves, understanding the good and the bad, attending nature's call, and many such simple things. Once these skills are instilled and introduced to the child at a tender age, it becomes easier to polish them and turn them into a gem. Elementary schools play a crucial role in enhancing these skills by engaging the child in various interesting social and physical activities that boost their confidence and make them smart and independent at the right age. Many times, kids tend to run away from the name of schooling and lose interest even before getting enrolled, as the concept of schools is presented in a very typical and monotonous manner to them. Thus, parents need to put in some effort to explore and figure out different entertaining ways to make the whole process of training their children a fun-filled venture.

Many times, busy working parents find it difficult to train their children and inculcate within them the required discipline, responsibility, self-esteem, positivity, and other key traits that are responsible for their healthy growth and development as an individual. There are many possible reasons why the healthy learning process in a child's life may be impacted, and parents must strictly consider these to enhance the quality of teaching they are imparting to their children. Thus, maintaining a healthy environment, providing emotional support, and acknowledging the child's achievements and efforts are a few quick tips to be followed by parents. The journey of preparing the little kids for school is an arduous one, as it is accompanied by numerous challenges and barriers that may come on the path of both parents and the children, compelling them to take a step back by discouraging them. However, with impeccable qualities within parents and different interesting approaches to training children, this whole process of teaching and learning can be made easier and smoother than ever.

Apart from this, it is also important for parents to be aware of what is correctly said about their children. Thus, parents must not always follow the crowd; instead, they should consider the needs, desires, and behavior of their children before believing or following any presumed fallacy that surrounds them and their children. On the whole, every step of raising a confident and independent child who is capable enough to go to elementary school with pride is not possible without the motivation and support of their parents. So, let's follow up each and every step of moving ahead with our children by teaching them the ABCs of different skills to make them happy and successful in their lives forever.

I hope this book helps you in gaining some perspective on how parents can help their pre-elementary age child begin their successful path to elementary school. If you found it helpful, I would deeply appreciate a positive review.

Chapter 1:

The First Step Toward

Learning

Everybody is a genius. But if you judge a fish by its ability to climb a tree, it will live its whole life believing that it is stupid. — Albert Einstein, a German Physicist

Education is one of the most vital assets that parents can gift to their children as it is considered to be a priceless wealth that one cannot afford to lose at any cost. The best thing about education, learning, and knowledge is that the more you share, the more it advances. Just as one can never go running without first learning how to walk, without gaining the basic knowledge imparted in elementary school, a child cannot progress further in their academic performance. Elementary education is the first step without which a child cannot climb the stairs of happiness and success, as it is the first stride that supports a child to make their dreams come true.

Most of us have a misconception that elementary school only teaches the academic skills that can help a child perform better in their school life. However, it is a place that lays the foundation for forming good and healthy habits that help children develop into their best selves through instilling life skills that teach them to survive on their own in any challenging circumstance. Elementary schooling provides a safe environment for the growth and development of a child by advancing their physical, emotional, mental, and social skills. However, many factors may impact the effectiveness of the learning process in an elementary school; thus, it is important for parents to extract the answers to the significant questions that help make this journey easy, enthusiastic, and exciting for both of them. So, let's dive deeper to answer all the important questions that can support parents to improve the learning experience for their children and guide them toward acquiring better knowledge and brushed-up skills.

Knowing About Elementary Education

In this dynamic world, where everyone is preoccupied with the struggle to improve their quality of life, education plays a very important role in building one's personality and identity as an individual. Education is the key to transforming one's life into a better and improved version, as it forms the base to impart the required knowledge, inculcate efficient skills, and uplift intellectual capacity in order to achieve the goals of life. However, developing these vital characteristics is not an overnight process; instead, it requires consistent and tremendous efforts from the very beginning and pointed in the right direction. The process of learning different things begins from the moment a child is born, like learning and understanding the language of communication and emotions, and recognizing one's parent's voice. Apart from all these, real teaching begins at a very young age when the child reaches the age of five to seven years old in the form of elementary education. Elementary education lays the foundation for a child to acquire knowledge, which is the fuel for evolving human life toward growth, developing new skills, improving memory, and keeping one mentally sharp.

Elementary education is also called primary education in some countries. The beginning age of elementary education in the United States is five to ten years old, which includes kindergarten and grades one to five. In elementary schooling, children are taught different subjects by one or various teachers in a single classroom. The major emphasized subjects are math, writing skills, critical thinking, reading, problem-solving, basic science, and social studies. It is not necessary to enroll your child into an elementary school directly, as there are preschools available that are meant for smaller kids aged two years up to five years old, where major emphasis is given to language, listening, basic math, vocabulary, and motor skills. Elementary education is followed by middle school, also called junior high school, which is for children aged eleven to thirteen years old, starting with grade six and going to grade eight.

Role of Elementary Education in a Child's Development

As we can never build a great building on a weak and faulty foundation, you can never expect a child who had an inadequate, lacking, and imperfect start to their education to achieve the bigger milestones in life. Elementary education is one of the prime investments parents can make for their children when they begin to grow up, as it will stay with them forever in the form of cognitive, socio-emotional, ethical, and physical development. When a child has a strong start during their elementary education, it increases the chances that they will perform better in the latter stages of their educational life and beyond that. So, let's dive deep and unveil the key roles that an elementary education plays in a child's development.

Teaches Moral Values

As a famous saying goes, "If wealth is lost, nothing is lost; if health is lost, something is lost; when a character is lost, all is lost." Similarly, moral values play a crucial role in determining a person's character and thus must be ingrained within a person from childhood itself. Just as healthy roots are responsible for growing healthy branches and leaves for a tree, developing strong roots of morals means ingraining good thoughts, which is the basis for having a healthy life ahead. Moral value is an important factor that guides a small child in the right direction to make apt decisions and gain acceptance and respect in society, which is fundamental for boosting self-confidence and staying strong. Elementary education is the best time and place for a child to learn these values, as along with basic teaching, they are taught the significance of honesty, kindness, equality, modesty, and respecting others and their opinions.

Inculcates Social Skills

When children are small, they learn to socialize with their parents and family only, which keeps them confined to a limited number of people and experiences. However, when entering into elementary education, a kid learns to communicate and socialize with many new people like teachers and other classmates. Elementary schools provide a whole new environment for young children, which helps in teaching them the act of sharing, playing, and interacting with each other. They grasp the skills of making new friends, helping each other, actively participating in play sports, group activities, and many new things.

Induces Physical Activity

Elementary school is the right platform for developing physical growth activities among small children. They are exposed to an environment where they play many new outdoor games like kickball, football, and tennis. This place is the best for one's physical growth and muscle strengthening. Running and playing new sports helps keep them fit and active, which also improves their quality of sleep and overall health.

Enhances Memory and Communication

An elementary school is a place where a kid experiences reading, writing, and interacting with many new faces for the first time. Participating in new activities like reading helps improve their visualizing and imaginary skills, which boosts memory power and stimulation. Furthermore, engaging in such fruitful activities also encourages them to converse with other classmates, which enhances their communication skills.

Boosts Self-Confidence

When a child enters into the elementary education phase, they grow in almost all spheres of their life, be it emotional, mental, or physical. They develop many new skills like the ability to communicate efficiently, play many outdoor and indoor games, learn new languages, make new friends, and also face ease in communicating, which all work toward making them feel more confident and proud of themselves. These skills not only teach self-confidence, they also make children feel worthy, thus enhancing self-esteem, which is an important requirement for a happy and healthy mindset.

Know the Perfect Age for Elementary Schooling

There are varied thoughts when deciding upon the perfect age for a child to enroll in an elementary school. For some parents, enrolling a kid in elementary school as early as possible is the key to improving their learning capabilities and helping them engage in productive and healthy habits. In such cases, parents believe that starting an elementary education at five years old or even younger, like four years old, is considered the best to set a strong foundation. However, this is not true in every case, as experts claim that when you start a child's schooling a bit later, like six years old instead of five, it helps in achieving better scores and showing improved learning and self-control (Weller, 2017). Psychologists believe that self-control is the executive foundation that supports a child to concentrate on their tasks, maintain focus, and budget their time even when they are faced with several distractions (Weller, 2017). Nonetheless, as every child is different, one can never decide when to start their elementary education based upon the ideal figures. So, let's have a look at the few signs that may help a parent to get a clear picture of whether their kid is ready for elementary school or not.

- Ability to understand and follow the instructions.

- Eagerness to interact and play with other children.

- Ability to express themselves easily in front of their peers and teachers.

- Gross motor skills like playing, balancing, and jumping.

- Fine motor skills like holding crayons and pencils, turning pages, etc.

- Having a good learning capacity and understanding ability.

Tips to Add Fun Into the Journey Toward Schooling

When a child enters the age of elementary education, they undergo mixed feelings while going to the school as there is a lot of pressure on these young minds. A child is small enough to express the rush of emotions like the anxiety of leaving parents, nervousness of meeting other children and teachers, or simply the fear of staying away from home. For whatever reason, if a child is not in a happy state of mind, it becomes a challenging task for them to sit in a classroom, learn, and take an interest in the activities. Thus, it is very important for parents and teachers to make this journey a fulfilling one for kids together. When learning becomes interesting, a child is automatically attracted to it, which eases the entire process of imparting the right and beneficial knowledge and skills to these young souls. So, let's explore the simple ways that can aid a parent to make this journey an exciting one for their kid.

Break Up the Session

Studying and learning a new lesson may seem to be a boring and hectic task for a small child, which could cause them to run away from books and classes. However, breaking the learning classes into sessions of 6 to 10 minutes and adding up fulfilled activities in between can help to engage a child for longer.

Give Them Choices

Most of the time, a small child is not given the chance to make their choices. Instead, they are levied with the instructions to do the task, which makes it quite boring for them to concentrate. However, when you open the doors of choices for your little bundle of joy, they start to develop an interest in learning. For instance, give them a choice to decide what lesson, subject, or homework they want to start with or try to add an entertaining activity of their choice.

Engage Through Games

Incorporating several online and offline games increases the instant engagement of a child in the lessons, which is an incredible way to drive their interest. Adding games into the teaching plans not only creates a fun element but also supports early learning and boosts the memorization power of young kids. Including games is also a simple thing for parents to do as there are extensive free online games available, which also saves preparation time.

Plan a Shopping Day

Plan a day out with your child to shop for the list of stuff required for their elementary school. Assist your child in selecting their new uniform, books, study table, pencil case, water bottles, shoes, socks, and many more things. Doing so would make them feel special and excited about the process of getting enrolled in school. Thus, shopping with your kid not only adds a fun element, it also prepares them mentally to participate in various activities by using their stuff when they go to school.

Customize the Study Room

A place that has attractive and colorful interiors is the best to engage a child in studies, especially when they are just beginning the journey of elementary education. Invest in customized stickers and wallpapers that can help in designing the interiors of their study room. Allow your kid to participate in the decoration process based on their likes and dislikes, as it would create a comfortable and friendly environment for them to study and spend most of their time learning and playing. Thus, try including a small whiteboard or blackboard with a duster, colorful chalks, board markers, alphabet and mathematical charts, and posters of their favorite cartoon engaged in studies and school activities.

Narrate Rhymes and Stories

Try creative activities like making them learn a few rhymes related to school and education to make it a refreshing, attractive, and fulfilling experience for them. Apart from rhymes, narrate short stories related to school and elementary education, which can raise their curiosity and excitement about the whole process. Singing rhymes and narrating stories also helps relax these young minds as it removes any pressure or stress from their mind by making the idea of schooling clearer and more familiar for them.

Motivate by Rewarding Them

Forcing a child to actively participate in going to elementary school and learning the lessons can be burdensome for both the parents and kids. However, adopting rewards, praise, and acknowledgment effectively encourages a child to behave in the desired and positive manner. But, one must be careful while doing so because if rewards are misinterpreted as bribery, it would negatively impact a child's attitude toward elementary schooling. Parents can use two types of rewards, either in the form of physical things like toys, chocolates, and candies, or social rewards like showing affection and appreciation, spending some precious time together at their favorite place, or engaging in their favorite sports and activities with them.

Ways to Prepare a Child for Elementary School

Entering a new phase of life is never an easy task for anyone, as it induces mixed feelings of excitement with lots of fear, anxiety, and nervousness. Similarly, for young kids, starting elementary school is a huge milestone in their development, which often fills their innocent minds with confusion, pressure, and hesitation. As no two children are alike, not every child will have the same feelings while going to elementary school. Some may show lots of excitement, curiosity, and happiness. However, parents play a crucial role in helping their children to feel comfortable and relaxed if they prepare them before sending them to elementary school. Some of the useful skills that a parent must impart to their child to make them feel confident before going to elementary school are:

Physical Skills

- By the time a child reaches the age of five years old, they are eligible for elementary school; thus, it is important to teach them the proper process of using toilets independently. These skills include the ability to dress and undress, wash hands, flush, and understand the importance of hygiene. By teaching toilet hygiene and skills, you can save your child from facing any embarrassment due to accidents.

- When a child enters elementary school, they are expected to eat their meal on their own along with a group of other children. Thus, it is important to encourage your child to eat independently without seeking any help from elders, which includes using cutlery, opening and closing the lunch box, and basic table manners.

- While in school, there may be a change in the weather that requires a child to take off an extra layer or jacket or put one on. Therefore, a child must be taught the simple ways to dress and undress themselves independently without being reliant on their parents. To make it easy, use jackets that have zips rather than buttons and shoes that have Velcro instead of laces.

Socio-Emotional Skills

- Prepare your child mentally to live in the company of others, as it helps develop their habit of living apart from their parents for some time. The best idea is to send your child to nursery, preschool, or other family members every day for a few hours.

- Make your child familiar with the school even before the session starts, as it helps them feel more comfortable and welcome once they join. When you visit the school with your child, it removes any kind of fear or concern that they have in their mind.

- Develop a habit of taking your child to public places like playgrounds where they can meet, play, and interact with many other children. Socializing with other children builds their confidence to initiate conversation or play with others. It also teaches the basic socializing skills of sharing and taking turns to avoid fights and practicing patience.

- Invest time to interact with your child as it helps them to develop a habit of expressing their feelings and problems so they can easily share their concerns and issues with teachers. This helps them to portray a more confident and independent attitude at school.

Academic Skills

- Encourage your child to participate in reading books by narrating the stories and discussing the characters. Once they develop an interest in reading, it becomes easy for them to follow up in school as well.

- Help your child to recognize their name through games or playful interactions with them. When a child goes to school, they must know how to differentiate between the belonging of other children and their things.

- Invest time to make your child learn counting through games, poems, and songs or by sending them to play schools. A child must know the counting and recognition of numbers from one to ten before going to elementary education.

- Help your child develop fine motor skills, including how to hold a pencil correctly. A parent can support a kid to learn this skill by practicing at home doing coloring or writing.

Information a Child Must Know Before Joining School

Joining an elementary school is a great milestone for a child that helps them learn and brush up on many important skills that form an integral part of their social, emotional, physical, and mental development. A child has full support from their parent, teachers, and family when they join an elementary school, but there are a few basic things that must be taught to them beforehand in order to ensure their safety and security. Thus, helping them gain knowledge and learn the necessary information about their parents, home, school, and community is a significant step before sending them to an elementary school. So, it is a must to develop and polish the following details, which are crucial for preparing a child for any kind of emergency in elementary school.

- Their full name.

- Name and phone number of their parents.

- Their complete home address.

- Their date of birth and place.

- Name and contact number of a close family member in case of an emergency.

- Any medical issues, allergies, or health problems they have.

- Knowledge of emergency numbers and the correct way to dial them.

Chapter 2:

Basic Life Skills a Child

Must Develop Before

Elementary Schooling

It is easier to build strong children than to repair broken adults.
—F. Douglas, an American Social Reformer

In this technologically revolutionized and data-driven world, every parent is keen to provide their child the best education that can make them taste success once they grow into an adult. However, one often forgets to emphasize the cornerstone of what makes them successful. Life skills are the revolutionary, path-breaking, and holistic way to impart the right knowledge and comprehensive education from the very beginning of a child's school life. Life skills are the essential building blocks for developing a child's understanding of how to apply the knowledge they acquire in school to real-life situations and problems. These are the skills that broaden the critical thinking ability of a small child, which is the first step to analyzing a problem from varied angles and finding feasible solutions. Inculcating such skills within a child at a young age supports them to become more independent not only in their approach but also in their thoughts, socializing skills, problem-solving, and making the appropriate choices at the right time.

However, most parents neglect this important factor and only focus on providing their kids with the best academic skills. This has created a huge gap between what we teach a child in the classroom and the life skills that are needed to accomplish real-life goals. Thus, parents and teachers need to realize the significance of imparting the lessons of life to train their children even before they enter elementary school, as these skills boost their ability to perform well not just in the classroom but also improve their overall lifestyle. So, let's have a look at the list of the few most important qualities that positively contribute to bridging the gap between traditional academic-based education and a holistic approach toward learning life skills.

Responsibility

Responsibility is a broad term that includes many aspects, like being dependable, keeping commitments, being accountable for your actions, and being able to make the right choices and decisions. Responsibility is an important characteristic that must be inculcated within a child when they are two or three years old. Developing this key trait within a child from a very young age strengthens their roots to success when they join an elementary school and even later in life when they grow up as an adult. As and when a child grows older, it becomes challenging for parents to instill the right skills within them as they develop habits, perceptions, and ideologies about many things in life. Thus, the best age to teach responsible behavior is when they begin to understand things and learn to take instructions properly.

Parents play a major role in imparting such skills to their kids as they are the prime support system and also the closest person to them. Every parent plays a dual role while dealing with a child. One role defines pure love, care, and nurturing, while the other one is an executive role where you set the limits and teach your child the proper ways to do things, which helps them to develop a sense of responsibility. Parents must levy age-appropriate responsibilities on their young kids, like asking a three-year-old to clean up their mess once they are done playing or seeking the help of a four-year-old to fold the piled-up clothes. Parents can even try hacks like asking them to complete time-bound goals like eating snacks on their own or trying to dress and undress themselves. Eventually, these instructions become habits which induce a sense of responsibility.

Respectful Behavior

Being respectful is one of the core values that a person can have as it lays the foundation for developing strong bonds and relationships with family, friends, and other people around them. Respectful behavior also teaches one to be kind, concerned, and considerate toward others, including strangers, which becomes the key to earning back respect and trust from other people too. As the famous saying goes, "Respect can never be asked for; it must be earned." Similarly, one can never get back respect unless they behave the same way with others. Portraying respectful behaviors gradually becomes a habit and part of one's character that others perceive as praiseworthy. Thus, the lessons of developing respectful behavior must be taught at a young age for children to grow into humble, polite, courteous, and kind human beings.

As parents are the very first teachers of their children, the lessons of respectful behavior begin at home ever since a child is small. Behaving respectfully is the basic skill that supports a child to make strong bonds and connections with their peers in elementary school. A respectful child receives praise and acknowledgments from their teachers and becomes an example for other children, too, which raises their self-esteem. Such positive acclaim and acknowledgment help a child develop an interest and participate in the activities of elementary school, which improves their overall performance. The first step to teaching a small child respectful behavior is to show respect toward them and avoid using any harsh tone or sarcastic and humiliating talk. You can never teach your kid to respect others by disrespecting them. Sometimes, when you notice your child behaving disrespectfully try to dig out the reason behind their behavior rather than confronting them as it would worsen the situation. Use polite and kind ways to teach your child and avoid punishing them by hitting or yelling. Apologize whenever you mess up or show rude behavior, as the best way to teach a child is by setting an example.

Empathy

We are familiar with an old saying, "Before you judge or criticize someone else, try walking a mile in their shoes," which clearly emphasizes the importance of empathy. Empathy is simply the ability to imagine, be aware of, or understand the experiences or feelings of others. Empathy lays the foundation for forming strong and positive relationships and friendships in life as it reduces the scope for misunderstanding and conflicts. Empathy encourages kindness, generosity, and helpful behavior and is the key ingredient for one to succeed in one's life. When a child lacks empathy, it can be concerning as they can indulge in unwanted and aggressive behavior, such as bullying, resulting in hurting other children. Further, a child who does not have empathic behavior faces extreme difficulty in making new friends and receiving help from others, which eventually results in disinterest in taking part in school activities. Thus, parents must analyze the behaviors of their children and reinforce the skills of empathy within them.

Teaching the lessons of empathy to a child is not an overnight process, as it requires time, effort, patience, and practice. A five-year-old is too small to understand exactly what it means to have empathy for others; therefore, parents must use a range of varied ways to build empathy within their kids. The best way to impart the right skills is to set an example by practicing empathic behavior toward your child. Read books and narrate stories that help them understand the feelings of others, use pretend play activities to teach them empathy lessons, and talk about their feelings and difficult emotions by naming them to help the child recognize and become familiar with them. You can also use the cutouts from books and magazines to show them the different emotions like sadness, anger, and happiness or help them learn to read body language by observing others.

Positive Self-Esteem

Self-esteem is a person's perception of themselves, their self-worth, and their belief in what they can do and achieve in life. Positive self-esteem is a pivotal quality that supports child development as it inculcates the confidence to try new things, even the ones that don't go according to plans, face challenges instead of avoiding them, bounce back, and do things they might not like or do at their own will. It is important to build positive self-esteem in children going to elementary school as they begin comparing themselves with other children. This impacts how a kid feels about themselves, performs in academics, participates in school sports and extracurricular activities, and also their ability to make friends. Thus, self-esteem is the governing factor that may impact the overall performance of a child in their elementary school life.

The beginning of elementary school welcomes new endeavors in a child's life. However, challenges in the form of poor grades or late submission of homework could dent their self-esteem and make them feel less worthy or more incapable than their peers. However, when parents invest time and effort into making a child realize that one does not need to be perfect in life to be valued, loved, capable, and successful, they start to develop positive self-esteem. Realistically, parents should support their children without being overprotective in order to raise the new generation of heroes with greater self-esteem and confidence. Acknowledge and praise a kid when they do a good job that needs applause and appreciation to teach them the importance of doing the hard work and being courageous to achieve success. Motivate a child when they try to do difficult tasks, even if they fail in the first attempt, to build their morale and resilience. Teach them through narrating moral stories that impart the lessons of positive self-esteem and its importance.

Active Listening

Childhood is a tender time that is not only filled with wonder and excitement but is also a great learning period responsible for cognitive, physical, social, and emotional development. Strong active listening skills lay a solid foundation for supporting a child to develop in all these four areas. Active listening is the ability to give undivided attention to the speaker by listening, understanding, and reflecting on what has been said. For a child going to school, active listening supports an improved understanding of concepts and learning as they can retain the lessons and refrain from getting distracted. Thus, active listening improves the effectiveness and efficiency of a child to learn what is being taught in the classroom. Apart from this, active listening also supports a child in making good friends, solving problems themselves, improving their communication, and also becoming more productive.

However, like all other life skills, even active listening is not a trait that a child is born with. Instead, parents are the prime teachers to inculcate active listening within their children, and they can lead by setting an example. Always practice active listening when you are talking to small children; give them importance and respect their words, and in return, they will do the same. Never interrupt a child when they speak, always make eye contact, and never ask a question when they are narrating a story or sharing their problems. You can also tell them stories to explain the importance of paying extreme attention when someone is talking, as it builds their understanding of active listening.

Self-Discipline

Most of us believe that disciplining a child simply means making them behave in a well-mannered and appropriate way. Many parents use punishments or harsh words to instill this habit within them. However, self-discipline is far away from what we do. Self-discipline is the ability of a child to manage and control their emotions like anger, make appropriate choices irrespective of their feelings, control their impulsive behaviors, and also show a respectful attitude toward their parents and teachers when they correct their mistakes. Self-discipline also supports a child to manage their schoolwork, homework, and time management and shows accountability for all their behaviors. A child who lacks self-discipline may face many issues, as they may often interrupt the teachers in the school while a class is going on or even show irresponsible behavior toward maintaining silence and decorum in the classroom. Exhibiting such non-tolerable behaviors could eventually lead them to face punishments and humiliation in class, which may impact their overall performance.

No child is born with an inbuilt quality of self-discipline; rather, it must be taught by the parents using varied useful ways. Parents must focus on setting proper routines and structure for their kids, as it helps them understand the value of doing the right things at the right time. For instance, have a routine for breakfast, getting dressed, bathing, lunch, nap time, and bedtime. Set rules, but always make it a point to explain the reason behind the rules to make it clear to a child about the pros and cons of following them. Sometimes, let your child learn through facing consequences, as once they learn a lesson, they become more conscious to never repeat the same, which teaches them self-discipline. Ensure that you take one step at a time, as developing such skills in a small child may take time, and rushing would make your efforts less effective.

Problem-Solving

When a child enters elementary school, it is obvious that they will meet new children and become friends with them. This is also, most of the time, followed by unwanted conflicts and problems among them. Sometimes, children may have differences of opinion, face negative peer pressure, or have disputes over their belongings. It is not always possible for a parent or teacher to be present and solve these issues for them. Thus, a child must be taught the skill of problem-solving from a very young age so they can easily find solutions to any problem they may encounter in their everyday lives. Problem-solving is a vital quality that induces confidence, independence, and creativity, improves academic performance, and also supports cognitive development. A child with problem-solving skills finds it easy to identify a problem early and prevent it from getting worse, which is the prime requirement for developing healthy and strong relationships with other children.

Parents can model problem-solving skills in front of their small kids to help them learn through live examples and feel that it's okay to have issues, but they must look for feasible options to deal with them. Whenever you have any issues, make it a habit to discuss and seek advice from your young kids, as it helps them understand that challenges are normal in their life. Invest time in talking to your child about the different emotions they face, be they good or bad, validate them by giving the emotions names, give them time to process those emotions, and allow them to find out the best solution. Also, narrate moral stories that help a child understand the importance of problem-solving, or even try creative play and activities that give them several opportunities to practice problem-solving.

Teamwork

A small child who has grown up confined within the four walls of their home with their parents alone would never learn the skills that help them to settle and engage in activities that involve more children. Teamwork is one of the most necessary skills that must be imparted to a child from a very young age as it forms the basis of developing all the other vital qualities. A child who is weak in building bonds with other children or lacks the ability to share and interact effectively faces many difficulties when they enter elementary school. Elementary school is a platform that needs a child to participate in various activities like team sports, group projects, group reading, arts and drawing, and puzzle solving. Teamwork helps in polishing other important characteristics like problem-solving, communication, self-esteem, creative thinking, leadership, and listening.

Parents can support a child to learn teamwork skills through many simple activities like helping them complete their homework, which improves their communication and also inculcates patience. Read stories together that emphasize the importance and benefits of teamwork to motivate your kid to practice the same at their school. Help build your child's confidence as a kid who portrays a reserved nature may struggle to collaborate in teams as they are scared to get walked over by other strong team members. Teach your child to practice fair play when in the team by following the rules, like showing kindness and taking turns. Encourage your child to be involved in sports activities and play games with other children living in the neighborhood to develop a habit of group bonding and socializing.

Balancing Emotions

The ability to manage and understand one's own emotions is the prerequisite for the appropriate development of a child. Children who have been taught the valuable skill of self-regulating their emotions portray responsible behavior by controlling their impulses, developing habits to express their emotions in a calm and controlled manner, and also by bouncing back after feelings of frustration, anger, or disappointment. Self-regulation is the key that supports the emotional and mental development of a child and is responsible for their improved academic performance, ability to make strong and healthy relationships, and independent behavior. A child who lacks the ability to balance their emotions often fails in their school life, as they tend to spoil their relationships with their school friends and could be a victim of bullying or boycotting at school. The inability of a child to regulate their negative emotions like anger, aggression, and withdrawal eventually leads to facing rejection at different steps of life, which becomes one of the biggest causes of dropping out of school.

Self-regulation is the secret to achieving great success in life as it helps in developing resilience, frustration tolerance, improved problem-solving abilities, and experiencing higher concentration and focusing skills, which form the basis to succeed in school and even in later life. The best way to teach self-regulation to a small kid is to provide a supportive framework to the child who is facing challenges to deal with their own emotions. Also, ensure to foster a positive and healthy emotional environment at home by modeling strong parent-child relationships and bonds between both parents and other family members. A positive environment is supportive in making a child feel secure and accepted, which helps in increasing the spectrum of their understanding of regulating emotions. You can also teach your kid coping skills to balance their emotions, like doing simple breathing exercises, counting to ten, or even redirecting one's attention to other positive things.

Chapter 3:

Factors That Impact Healthy Learning in Children

You cannot make people learn. You can only provide the right conditions for learning to happen. —Vince Gowmon, an American Writer

Most of us believe that sending our little five-year-olds to school is the major task that transforms them into highly intellectual human beings when they grow up and will make their life a lot easier and smoother. To make this happen, we explore and let our children enter a renowned elementary school where they can get the best education, which would adorn their lives with the bright, shining stars of knowledge and understanding. However, we ignore the most important requirement that can make this entire process happen effectively. Learning is a pivotal part of education, without which our children cannot prosper in their academics or later life. Learning is an art that must be taught from a very young age because the lessons of childhood leave the strongest impressions that stay with us in our memory forever.

Learning is a phenomenon that cannot be taught simply by asking a child to do so. Instead, it demands a perfect, empowering, positive, and supportive environment for a young kid to learn. A parent alone cannot direct the minds of their children toward learning. Instead, it calls for a list of impactful elements that control the learning process for them. Thus, every parent must explore the basic components that altogether assist a child in learning. So, let's dive deeper to unveil and understand the crucial factors that help a parent build up a favorable environment for their children to adapt to the process of learning.

Good External Atmosphere

As children grow up, they begin to understand the environment around them. However, for young kids, their parents and real-life experiences at home are the first major stepstones that leave a strong impression on their minds. The budding mind of a child is as pure as the driven snow; however, the journey of life will begin to carve their experiences, which gradually impacts their day-to-day working, emotional, and thought process. Research claims that a free-minded, relaxed mental state and a happy inner self is the most important requirement for a small child to prosper in the learning process (Desai, 2020). However, when parents are negligent and unaware of the importance of maintaining a healthy environment at home, they may end up creating a stressful, depressing, and negative mindset for their child, which eventually impacts their interest in participating in learning and other extracurricular activities. Therefore, parents must be conscious of discussing serious matters of concern or their conflicts at home in front of a child. Instead, parents must focus on showcasing a warm and welcoming attitude toward each other, which helps in keeping the child's mind free and relaxed. Providing an atmosphere that is free of any acrimony and tension and instead filled with happiness, love, and tranquility helps serve a child's welfare and interest in the best way where they prosper and achieve their goals successfully.

Emotional Support by Parents

Parents are the real lifelines for small kids as they need their support for doing everything. The role of a parent begins even before a child is born when they are in her mother's womb. Motivational words and life lessons taught by a parent to their child stay with them and continue to illuminate their life with courage and positivity when the shadows of darkness and hopelessness surround them. The power of prenatal support is everlasting. It helps a child perform beyond their limits and reach their goals. Similarly, for a small kid who begins the journey of elementary school, parental emotional support can do wonders and help them get over the various challenges that may come in their path. Emotional support of parents refers to their acceptance, responsiveness, warmth, attention, involvement, and support. A parent who is often involved in the everyday tasks and activities of their kid, who actively listens to their problems and concerns without being judgmental, comforts them in their sorrows, and gives them the affection they need helps in creating an emotionally sound and relaxing environment for their child. Further, supportive parents also ensure that their child is feeling safe, praise and acknowledge their minute efforts to encourage them, and use creative ideas to create opportunities for them to relax and play, thus having a great positive impact on their mind, eventually boosting their capabilities to learn and grow in life.

Capability of the Child

Most of us believe that there is a perfect age at which a child starts to learn and grow in their capabilities. However, a child's learning process begins from the time they take their first breath in this world. A child living safely in the mother's womb is unaware of the breathing process, but as they enter into this world, they cry hard, which expands their lungs, and they learn how to breathe. So, the process of learning is not a new concept for a small child. Learning is the process that requires a child's mind to behave inquisitively and actively, which supports critical thinking about complex and insightful issues. Cognitive ability is the capability of a child to process the information and thoughts that are present in their mind, which forms the basis for improving their learning process. In simple words, the learning and capabilities of a child, like cognitive ability and critical thinking, go hand in hand as they complement each other and cannot happen without the presence of the other. As parents are the closest being to a child, they know the best ways to enhance the capabilities of their kid by encouraging and progressing them toward learning. Parents must also try brushing up a child's life skills, helping them participate in new, innovative, and creative games and activities, and teaching them decision-making skills from a young age, thus raising a child with incredible and unbeatable capabilities that help them excel in life and achieve success.

Health Status of the Child

Most parents often focus on the external capabilities, strengths, and skills of a small child to help them enhance their personality. However, learning and success largely depend upon what a person is feeling from the inside. As a famous saying goes, "A healthy outside starts from a healthy inside." Similarly, when a child is free from mental distraction and physical discomfort, it opens up the gates toward a calm and relaxed mind, which forms the basis for improved learning. The prime requisite for developing good physical health in a child is to build healthy eating habits and food hygiene. Parents must focus on incorporating a routine for their growing children comprising of the three important meals of the day, which must include a mix of healthy and balanced diets. A nutritious diet contains sources of protein, carbohydrates, fats, vitamins, and minerals, which can be derived from different sources like poultry, fresh fruits, vegetables, legumes, fish, and nuts. However, even if a child consumes a healthy diet, minimal physical activity can cause childhood obesity and other health-related problems; thus, a child needs to do regular exercises and practice yoga, which helps keep them fit and active. Apart from this, parents must also emphasize providing a healthy external environment to a child to ensure their normal mental health. When the mind of a child is free from stress, tension, and worry, they feel positive, happy, and confident about themselves and the things going around them. Further, developing healthy habits within a kid, like practicing meditation to calm the mind and body and repeating positive affirmations when they feel low, stressed out, and anxious, helps to uplift their mood and also fills them with hope so they can perform their best in every sphere of life.

Child's Ability to Focus

As soon as a child enters elementary school, they are expected to engage in long stretches of classes where concentration plays a crucial role in helping them understand and learn. As they grow up, children are expected to participate in extracurricular activities after school time, which demands more attention and focus. The ability to focus is an important requirement for every child to help them perform well in their academics. While very few children are born with this amazing ability to focus, it is a skill that can be inculcated into a small child with practice, determination, and consistent efforts. Parents can support their kids by helping them adopt learning strategies and engaging in practices that improve their concentration and also sustain attention for a long.

While focusing on an interesting and enjoyable task is quite easy for most children, when a task seems boring, like long lectures or detailed lessons, it can be difficult for them to concentrate. However, developing the important skill to focus on every task, be it interesting or boring, helps a child to achieve good results, which improve their overall performance and boost their confidence and self-esteem. Parents must support their young kids to practice mindfulness as it is the core that helps one to focus on the current moment. Set a timetable for your child to do their homework in a separate room that is free from any distractions or television noise to help them maintain their concentration. Also, make it a habit to give them time-bound assignments and homework that help them learn to memorize and understand within a limited time. Do not burden a child with multiple tasks at a time, as they get confused and lose their focus. Apart from this, a good sleep pattern and a healthy diet are the basis that helps in improving a child's focusing ability.

Intelligence of the Child

Intelligence is the ability of a child to think, easily adapt to a new situation or environment, gain knowledge and learn from experiences, make decisions, and solve problems. It is an important factor for enhanced learning in a child. Fortunately, some children are gifted with intelligence, which is exhibited by their ability to learn, grasp, and understand school education. However, parents can support their small children who face issues with learning and struggle to improve their academic performance to increase their intelligence. You can easily grow your child's intelligence by giving them challenging situations to handle on their own and letting them solve tricky puzzles without giving hints. Several memory training activities like crosswords, Sudoku, jigsaw puzzles, and many more are extremely beneficial for improving memory, language skills, and reasoning, which form a significant part of intelligence. Encourage your child to engage in executive control activities like brainteasers, Pictionary, Scrabble, etc., which brushes up their decision-making skills, organizing, managing, and orienting abilities. Apart from this, visuospatial reasoning is at the core of helping to improve a child's intelligence, as the main focus is on enhancing one's mental processing power by looking at visual and physical representations. For instance, point-of-view activities, mazes, unfolded prisms, and 3-D models are the best activities to promote visual and spatial training in a child, thus increasing their intelligence.

Will of the Child to Learn and Explore

We are aware of a famous old saying that when you lose the willpower to achieve goals, it's obvious that you meet failures. The will to do something in life is the biggest strength of a person that compels them to resist their short-term temptations and move toward achieving their long-term goals in life. Willpower plays an important role in the life of students as it empowers them with self-discipline and self-control, which are the key to driving them toward success. Similarly, when five-year-olds start going to school, their willpower to study, focus, participate, and enjoy the process is the only driving force that helps them learn the lessons and explore. When children are young enough, they do not understand the significance of willpower; thus, parents play a major role in molding them into someone who takes an interest in their academic goals and works toward achieving them. Sometimes, learning seems to be a challenging task for some children, which makes them run away from the process. However, when supportive parents inculcate a strong feeling of willpower within them by explaining the importance of this powerful tool, they become unstoppable in life. Willpower is a competent skill that helps a child to face any new task, challenging thing, or problematic situation with hope, courage, and determination to strive through it without fearing defeat. It triggers the fire within a child, which helps them fight against all odds to overcome the negativities, stay focused, and choose the good habits over the bad ones. Thus, willpower is the most potent weapon in the armory of small children that makes them invincible and helps them proceed toward the fulfillment of their life goals.

Level of Motivation Given by Parents

Starting elementary school is an altogether new and difficult experience for a small child. They have many fears and concerns going on in their little mind, which keep pulling them back now and then. In such situations, when a parent firmly holds their little hands, hugs them tight, and says, "I know my darling, you are a strong child, and I believe in your efforts, you can do it," it can act as a game changer for them. Children are small, innocent beings who have no experience or knowledge of this world. All they know and learn is from their parents and their empowering words. When a parent makes a child believe in their capabilities, strengths, and skills, they begin to feel significant, masterful, and involved. This powerful weapon is called motivation. Motivation is not only about talking positively with your child; rather, it is hidden in the small gestures, words, and activities of day-to-day life that work wonders for cheering them up and filling them with the required momentum to move them toward success. Parents can motivate their kids in many simple ways simply by giving them their precious time to make them feel valued and build a strong connection with them. Whenever your child endeavors to achieve their goals, praise their efforts with positive and inspiring words, even if they fail in that attempt, to make them realize the importance of working hard rather than just achieving the outcomes. Every child is unique. Therefore, for some kids, giving them the authority and right to choose motivates them, while for others, challenging them with an achievable goal can do the needful. Thus, there is a list of innovative techniques and wonderful approaches that can support parents in filling their child with positive motivation that carves their path towards better learning and gaining excellence in life.

Financial Status of the Parents

For adults, money is the source for reaching their goals, fulfilling aspirations, and also having security in life. Money and financial status hold much value for an adult as it is responsible for achieving one's necessities like a home, healthcare, and food. For some, money is a valuable asset as it helps them fulfill their luxurious desires, like affording fancy cars and vacations. However, less known and understood by most of us, the financial status of parents plays a key role in the learning and development of a small child. As life is not black and white in all spheres, so is the role of the financial status of parents in a child's educational life. No doubt, when a parent can afford a good educational platform, books, a tidy uniform, and all the other requirements for a child's education, it motivates and inspires them to do better. However, children whose parents have limited access to financial resources may compromise with everything in life, like using second-hand books and uniforms for going to school, which impacts their mindset. When parents do not have financial stability, a child not only suffers physically but can also experience a strong negative mental and emotional impact, drastically affecting their academic performance and learning capabilities. Many thoughts run into the mind of these young budding souls, as at times they feel anxious to help their parents by using any means, while at other times they feel embarrassed for not being able to afford the same thing as their classmates. These factors affect them mentally and keep them preoccupied, causing stress and shame, which restricts their learning and effective participation in school events. It can also stop them from socializing with other children at school.

Educational Background of the Parents

Every parent, whether highly qualified or not, dreams of raising a child who excels in their academics, learns well, and succeeds in all the endeavors of life. Parental support is a pivotal requirement for a child as they are their biggest motivator and guide. However, when parents are not highly qualified or lack a strong educational background, they may fail to show the right path to their young kids. For one to educate and guide a child in the right direction, it is very important to have detailed knowledge and ideas about new tools and techniques to impart the best learning skills to them. The educational background of parents is an important factor that can flip the learning game for a small child. In the current era of highly advanced science and technology, there are tremendous new ways, tricks, and gadgets that can help children gain apt knowledge, which boosts their learning. Five-year-olds are not grown up enough to help themselves; thus, they turn to their parents for everything. When a parent has strong educational background, they are knowledgeable and aware of the new hacks and creative ideas that can enhance a child's learning process by making the process easier and simpler for them to understand. Therefore, well-educated parents can show better parental behaviors and emotional support, which is the prime requirement for cultivating learning and habits that directly affect a child's academic performance. While parents cannot go back and make changes to their educational background, there is always scope to improve and upgrade one's awareness and grasp the relevant information about the new and improved ways to boost a child's learning capacity.

Chapter 4:

Challenges While Training a Child for Elementary School

Children are not things to be molded but are people to be unfolded. —Jess Lair, a Renowned Writer

Life has never been perfect for any one of us, as one day you might feel perfectly awesome and sorted out, while the next morning could raise anxiety and fears within you. In simple words, challenges are part and parcel of life that carry a huge meaning for each one of us. Unless we get into problems, we never strive to find out more feasible and effective ways that could make things work for us. Living simply with a relaxed mind would never push us toward perfection or to make efforts to improve our lifestyle. When there are challenges, we leave no stone unturned to resolve them. Similarly, as our child grows up, we realize both of our lives are full of tricky tasks, be it teaching them life skills, inculcating the right eating habits, giving them potty training at the right age, or simply preparing them for elementary school. We all face challenges, but how we deal with these situations is what matters and defines the path to our destiny.

Life bestows upon us endless challenges, which we have to deal with on our own by learning the appropriate and effective ways. Developing skills and techniques that can help in facing these obstacles make us stronger, more confident, centered, and calm even in a panic situation. Therefore, it is important to identify and understand the various difficulties that come in the way of parents and children when the latter starts going to elementary school, as it could make it easy for one to mentally prepare themselves and contemplate feasible ways to transform the situation into a better one. So, let's scrutinize and unveil the unexpected road bumps that may unexpectedly pop up and impact the morale of parents and children as they begin the journey of enrolling their little kids into an elementary school.

Barriers on the Parent's End

In today's busy and work-oriented world, sparing quality time for oneself is a big challenge. So, when it comes to investing some precious time with your loved ones and your children, it can seem to be an arduous task for most parents. Since the mind of a child is like a blank canvas that needs to be painted beautifully with attractive colors, we as parents must put in some effort and time to do the needful. At such a gentle age, a child needs their parents' utmost attention, as they want them to explain every minute detail required for initiating the learning of any new skill. However, this often becomes a tiring task for an exhausted parent who has been struggling throughout the day with the household chores, managing the home, and balancing their professional and personal life.

There are many sources of distraction in the path of small children, as they are busy exploring the things around them and thus can give a tough time to parents in the journey of learning the ABCs of various fundamental skills of life. But, with immense willpower, patience, and love toward our children we can beat the odds and be successful in training our children in the basic knowledge and skills required to take their first step toward achieving wisdom and perceiving their lives in a better way. Therefore, it is important to identify and understand the barriers that come in the way of training a small child, as it can improve parents' awareness and prepare them mentally to manage the challenges and problems. So, let's explore the various issues that may restrict a parent from inculcating the essential survival skills in their kids for starting with elementary education.

Explaining Schools' Rules and Guidelines

Elementary school is altogether a new experience for small children where they are supposed to learn the rules and guidelines themselves, as a parent can no longer support them when they go to school. This is a common point where most parents face issues, as explaining the dos and don'ts of school to these young minds takes much longer. Some children have higher understanding levels and memory power, so it is easy for them to grasp these guidelines. However, a kid who has a lower maturity level would tend to forget, ignore, or show irritable behavior toward understanding these rules. Apart from this, most children are distracted due to other things like games, screen time, and playing with other kids, which makes it a challenging task for parents to explain these rules to them. However, parents must keep trying different interesting ways to help their children learn the basic regulations of their school. For instance, you can try giving examples of other children like older siblings and friends who have excelled in following the rules and have earned huge appreciation from parents and teachers. Motivating a small child by citing examples, listing the pros and cons, or narrating moral stories can also do the needful.

Imparting Safety Training

Sending your ward to elementary school for the first time is an overwhelming task as it needs a big heart to send them to a place where you can no longer look after them. Because we as parents cannot be with them at every stage of their school life, it is a big matter of concern to teach these young souls the safety rules. Safety training not only helps a parent to stay relaxed and stress-free, but it also prepares small children to protect themselves against any unfortunate incident occurring at school. Imparting the safety training helps in making children aware of the possible dangers and accidents that they may face at school without making them fearful and nervous. However, many obstacles come when you teach your kid about the safety rules. For example, it is quite challenging for small children to memorize the contact details of their parents and their complete home address.

Apart from this, it is difficult for parents to ensure that a child will follow the taught rules and emergency tips. Sometimes, when engaged in the play, a child may exit the school premises to pick up a ball or simply enter a pool or go to a bus without any supervision or having teachers around. Nonetheless, getting distressed and anxious is never the solution, as one must keep trying and teach their child to have a strong mindset about following the safety rules.

Inculcating Hygiene Habits

The immunity of a small child is not as strong as that of an adult. A child who has poor sanitization and unhygienic habits is prone to catching an illness that disrupts their overall lifestyle. Developing healthy hygiene habits within a small child supports enhancing their physical, mental, emotional, and social well-being. Children who practice good hygiene habits over time have a better perception of themselves. This boosts their confidence and self-esteem, which is the basis for making new friends and building strong bonds with other children in school. Some of the important hygiene habits include toilet hygiene, like having the skills to use the washroom on their own without the support of others, and food hygiene, like washing their hands before and after eating and wiping their face after each meal.

Apart from this, hand hygiene includes keeping their fingers and nails clean each time they play outdoors and come back home from school, and oral and body hygiene, which is about bathing daily, brushing their teeth, and many more. However, the major hindrance in the path of teaching such hygiene habits is the resistance of a child to follow these habits as routine, over-indulgence in games and other distractions, or inability to grasp these skills easily. When a child is young, they are dependent upon their parents for everything, but entering elementary school creates the urgency to inculcate these habits as their everyday routine, which they must do on their own. However, just as practice makes perfect, similarly, putting in consistent efforts and using creative ideas can help a parent make their child learn these habits.

Handling Indifferent Behavior of Children

It is normal for young kids to experience a range of varied emotions due to which they express themselves in different ways. While a child is in the developing stage, they exhibit behaviors like irritability, breaking rules, and throwing tantrums at parents, which can make it difficult for a parent to handle and train them. The most common behavioral issues that hinder the endeavor of parents are defiance, where they refuse to listen and understand your viewpoint; showing extreme anger when they feel they are not being heard and understood; fussiness, especially when you try to teach them good manners and healthy habits; and hurting others which may raise issues in school like bullying other children, hitting, biting or kicking them. There are many reasons for a child to behave in such challenging ways; either they are slow at learning emotional and social skills, or they are looking for their parent's attention. However, the only way to deal with these indifferent behaviors of small kids is to invest time into understanding them. Once you get to know the exact reason behind your child's indifferent attitude, it becomes easier to tackle the issue by correcting their behaviors to avoid them in the future, which is the prime requisite for making them learn healthy habits.

Reducing Distraction

With so many advanced gadgets and technically driven education systems available, it is not easy for a young kid to stay attentive for long. One of the biggest distractions of the current era is the extensive availability of the internet, mobile phones, and the overindulgence in screen time. Nowadays, it has become a common view to find every child involved in using smartphones and other electronic devices on their own. Apart from this, several other factors also affect a child's attention, like lack of sleep, unhealthy eating habits, stress, depression, or anxiety. A small kid gets stimulated by every single noise, color, shape, and object, making it hard for them to concentrate on one thing at a time. For instance, a child easily loses focus while learning a rhyme and begins to fidget with their pencil or starts looking at the view outside the window.

Distractions are a major concern that blocks a parent's path to inculcating the right skills necessary for a child to enter elementary school. Almost every skill that is crucial for a child entering elementary school needs their concentration. Be it any complex attention-related skills like reading, memorizing, writing, or language learning, lack of focus disturbs the entire process of training a child. However, just as every lock has its key, there are plenty of simple, easy, and practical ways that can support a parent to improve the attention of their child. For instance, motivate your kid to practice meditation as it boosts focusing ability and also removes stress or invest time and pay much attention to reading to your child as it helps boost the parent-child relationship and also improves their concentration level. Other important tricks are to manage their screen time, encourage them to play focus games, emphasize sleep hygiene, appreciate their efforts, and provide them with a healthy diet to reduce their distractions.

Challenges Faced by Children

For a small child, life is no less than a roller coaster ride, as they feel a list of different emotions now and then. Some could be associated with happiness and comfort, but others may be stressful and depressing. While feeling stressed out is part of life, and it can happen to anyone at any stage of life, feeling stressed is not strictly a negative emotion, as it doesn't only occur when something bad happens to us. When the situation or environment is changing for small kids or they start a new chapter of their life, they may feel stressed out. As we cannot prevent a child from feeling such emotions, we must put in the effort to understand the situation that is affecting our kids and teach them effective ways to face those challenges. Similarly, when a small child enters elementary school, they have several things going in their mind that impact them emotionally and physically. Thus, parents need to have a detailed idea about the various thoughts, problems, and dilemmas that children face when they begin their new journey of life. So, let's have a look at the various challenges young children can face that can impact their morale, determination, and enthusiasm to learn and participate in productive activities.

Separation Anxiety

For a small child, the safest and warmest place in this world is near to their parents at home. However, when a child begins to grow up and reaches the age of going to an elementary school, their mind wanders in many directions. Separation anxiety is one of the biggest fears and concerns ingrained into their innocent minds. It is not easy for young kids to stay away from their parents and spend a few hours alone in the company of strangers and unfamiliar people. Separation anxiety is a common issue among growing children, which often hinders their learning process as they are not able to concentrate on their academic goals. Separation anxiety is not a permanent feeling; rather, it fades away with time as and when a child grows up and learns about their surroundings and new people in school. Parents must invest time in understanding their children by talking to them, practicing active listening, and also paying attention to their feelings. Practice strict routines, even on the weekends, by letting them play and engage in activities with friends and trusted family members for some time away from home, as it helps them to adjust easily. Narrate moral stories to encourage and motivate them to stay happy and enjoy school life without parents, which helps them to get over the separation anxiety.

Difficulty in Communication

Communication is the key to productive interaction with another person. It entails four components: listening, writing, reading, and speaking. Developing communication skills is a prerequisite when a child enters elementary school. However, it is not easy for every child to excel in these four components. There are several reasons why a child may have difficulty developing apt communication skills. Some children may have a slow developmental growth rate, face issues in taking instructions and expressing their thoughts, lack confidence and fear facing new people, are unable to remember things for long, or have autism spectrum disorder issues. Sometimes, when a child is overexposed to smartphones and other gadgets, they interact with others less. In such cases, the development of communication skills is quite slow in a child. The best way to deal with such challenges is to give time to a kid to grasp, learn, and respond to any instruction and by helping them to build new and useful vocabulary that supports them in opening up effective communication. Help your child by providing them with some icebreakers that can help them make new friends at school, like, "What is your name?" "What is your favorite cartoon?" or "Can we play together?" Moreover, one should also invest sufficient time to teach them school-related words like bell, assembly, playground, etc., or useful sentences and phrases to ask for help from teachers and friends.

Adopting a New Routine

As a famous saying goes, "The only thing constant is change." Similarly, the journey of life is full of transitioning from one phase of life to another, which forms the basis of growth, development, and accomplishment of new goals. Likewise, in the life of a small child, transitioning from a stay-at-home lifestyle or a preschool into an elementary school is a significant milestone. Yet, it can be a demanding task as it is not easy for them to adapt to an entirely new environment with a happy and smiling face. Entering an elementary school brings with it many emotional and physical challenges for a small kid, like leaving their home, meeting new people, feeling nervous, anxious, and sad about separating from their family, and getting out of their comfort zone. For a small child, even a slight change in their routine is scary that upsets them, be it moving to a new house, having a new pet, leaving old friends, or welcoming a new baby. However, parents can support their children and prepare them for the change by setting new routines, rescheduling things, and talking to them about the change and elementary school. Furthermore, teaching them life skills like accountability and independence by making them participate in the entire process, like packing bags, setting out their clothes, deciding on the lunch menu, and many more, can develop their interest and enthusiasm, helping to get rid of the resistance toward adopting a new routine.

Managing Peer Competition

Encouraging peer competition is an important topic of debate that is not only applicable to teenagers but also to children going to elementary school. A child entering elementary school lacks experience and knowledge about peer competition, and they often fail to manage stress and pressure and begin comparing themselves with other students. Like every coin has two sides, peer competition also has a positive as well as a negative end. Developing a healthy peer competition can help motivate a child to give their best and achieve the desired results, which could support the kids to excel in their studies. However, when a child misunderstands the concept of peer competition, it may result in jealousy, toxic habits like pushing beyond the limits, which results in stress and anxiety, and negative competition where a child tries to put others down to achieve their goals. It is not easy for young children to understand the power of peer competition, and thus, they struggle to improve themselves as they become overindulged in putting others down. Therefore, parents must counsel their children to make them understand the meaning, importance, and benefits of managing peer competition at school. The elementary school sets down the basic structure of education for small children; thus, it is important to correct their concepts to help them grow fruitfully and positively. A young child's mindset eventually becomes stronger as and when they grow, which makes it highly challenging for one to transform later in life. Therefore, parents must give utmost attention to teaching the right skills for managing the peer pressure their children will experience once they enter elementary school.

Making New Friends

Making and keeping new friends is an innate human characteristic that starts ever since childhood, and it is the key to evolving and getting into warmer relationships with people around us. When a child enters elementary school, they are exposed to an open environment where they meet hundreds of new children, and fortunately, they become friends with a few of them with whom they are most compatible. Making new friends is good for the emotional and mental development of a kid as it boosts self-confidence and self-esteem and also brushes up their socialization skills. However, not every child is blessed with the ability to make friends instantly and face major challenges which begin to impact their emotional well-being. It is a sad, upsetting, and embarrassing feeling for young kids when they are unable to make good friends. Eventually, it overshadows their confidence and willingness to interact with other children. The inability of small children to make friends is a clear sign that they lack efficient social skills. Thus, parents must pay attention to their child's activities and skills when they start going to school, and also by interacting with their teachers to enquire if the child is doing well in school with other classmates. Having an awareness of the child's social skills makes it easy for parents to teach them the right tricks to start a conversation and keep it going, respond to social cues, listen to other children, understand them, and interact in a positive way which helps in instilling the quality in a kid to make good friends throughout their life.

Learning New Subjects

When a child reaches the age of elementary school, they are expected to be able to recognize the alphabet, numbers, and shapes, hold crayons and pencils, color different pictures, and make slanting, sleeping, and straight lines. However, as they enter elementary school, the burden of the syllabus to learn, recognize, write, and speak increases dramatically, creating challenges for a small child to learn and memorize. For instance, the main syllabus in an elementary school begins by focusing on writing uppercase and lowercase alphabets, writing three-letter words, learning and writing numbers, basic addition and subtraction, and many other subjects like learning shapes, colors, time, and seasons. Although the focus of every teacher and the curriculum of the schools is to start slow to help a child learn with ease, many kids still lag.

Several factors impact this slow learning ability of the child, like the inability to focus, being easily distracted by other ongoing activities, disinterest in repeating things at home, unhealthy sleep and eating patterns, or a parent's negligence to focus on their child's abilities and polish them. Sometimes factors like lower motivation, absence of appreciation and rewards, or mental issues like stress due to issues at home like disputes between parents, the financial burden on family, etc., also have negative effects on the learning ability of a kid. However, parents can help their child by unearthing the underlying cause of the child's poor learning abilities, as it helps in sorting out the issues that can remove the barriers that restrict them from excelling in elementary education. Further, parents must have a detailed conversation with the teachers to understand the problems with their young kids or try creative and innovative methods of making them learn the lessons. Apart from this, parents must stop over-emphasizing reading the lessons to their children every time they are engaged in some playful activity, as it starts to become a burden for them, which in turn could cause them to flee from their studies.

Chapter 5:

Perks of Preparing a Child

Before Elementary

Schooling

If parents want to give their children a gift, the best thing they can do is to teach their children to love challenges, be intrigued by mistakes, enjoy effort, and keep on learning. —Carol S. Dweck, an American Psychologist

We all are born to serve a purpose in our lives, for which we need some or the other pivotal skills that prepare us to face problems and strive toward accomplishing our desires and aspirations. These critical traits are fundamental in that they form our support system throughout our life's endeavors. As none of us are born with these unique skills, the process of developing these indispensable characteristics must begin at a very young age. It is because the lessons learned in the initial days of our lives are deep-seated ones that leave an intense impression on our minds. Therefore, it is necessary to inculcate the most admirable, effective, and effervescent qualities within a small child from a very young age, as it is the basis for making them confident and courageous enough to set higher goals and work hard with determination to achieve them. Elementary schooling is one such phase in the life of young children, which provides them with a wide platform to learn and imbibe the vital qualities that prepare them mentally, emotionally, and physically to take a step closer to their dreams.

Elementary education is the basic right of every child, and parents must put in consistent efforts to support their kids by preparing them before enrolling them in school, throughout the journey, and even beyond that. Nowadays, with the advancement of technology and adoption of a wide range of versatile teaching styles, the purpose of an elementary school is not only confined to instilling basic education and boosting academic performance, but they have an objective of training a child in the best possible manner to hone their overall personality. So, let's explore the diverse ways in which training a child before elementary schooling can add glitters of magical essence to their life.

Builds Patience

We live in a world where instant gratification has become the current norm, and setting the right examples in front of our young children has become the need of the hour so that they behave in the same manner. Practically speaking, it is quite common to see the frustration and impatience on the faces of adults when their parcels take a bit longer to arrive or if it takes more than a few seconds to send a text to someone. Similarly, it is the new normal to witness a child crying and getting irritated when their video games take longer to load or when any of their wishes are not fulfilled immediately. Nowadays, things in our surroundings have changed dramatically, which affects not only mature adults but also young budding souls, too. In such circumstances, patience is a deep-rooted word that holds immense value and stance for each one of us, as it is fundamental to boosting mental, physical, and social health. Patience works like a booster, which automatically reduces the negative feelings of psychological stress and other physical health-related issues like blood pressure and increased heart rate, thus making us feel relaxed. It is a trait that teaches us the art of being in our calm and controlled state, irrespective of the external abyss going on in our surroundings. Patience not only fills our lives with joy, positivity, and improved decision-making, but it also enhances our social skills. It is observed that a person who practices patience is more likely to have a good, honest, and committed relationship in life.

Considering all this, it is very normal for a small child to exhibit irritable, restless, and moody behavior when their needs are not met. However, no one in this world is born with the inbuilt quality of being patient, and this has to be inculcated in one's personality right from the beginning. The best time to instill the transforming quality of patience within our little children is when we prepare them to face the challenges of elementary school, which can effectively help to manage their behavior and equip them with basic survival life skills. We need to sow the seeds of this noble trait within our children before they are exposed to this world, and the rest is taken care of by the elementary schools, which play a major role in carving the path for our children by teaching them discipline, mindfulness, controlling their impulses, following a specific schedule, and imparting consciousness toward their behavior. Apart from this, elementary schools also provide a proper space where every kid gets an opportunity to interact with and understand other children with patience. Thus, instills within them the spirit of teamwork, collaboration, problem-solving, empathetic behavior, and also a helping attitude, thereby making them more patient in order to deal with difficult and challenging situations optimistically.

Inculcates a Positive Attitude

There is an old saying that emphasizes the fact that having an optimistic mindset and determination is stronger and more effective than simply putting in hard efforts, as it can make even an impossible task possible. Our attitude and perspective toward different things, challenges, and critical situations are what define our success or failure in the end, as it's all a mind game. This, in turn, governs and directs our thought process, which eventually impacts our happiness, comfort, and contentment. It inculcates the feeling of hopefulness, optimism, and enthusiasm to take up any task, be it simple or tricky. It provides us with the confidence to meet new people, make friends, and gain new experiences in life without sparing a moment in a dilemma. Achieving a positive attitude transforms our lives as it sets a growth mindset that helps in fighting against draining emotions like helplessness and cynicism that various negative events happening around us can ingrain into our minds. Moreover, having an optimistic outlook filters the feelings of dissatisfaction and despair, which opens up new opportunities and makes it easy for one to choose the path of success by facing the worst hurdles. Thus, inculcating a positive attitude that gives rise to a growth mindset is important for the healthy development of small children as well. Being adults, we have a cluster of knowledge and awareness that helps us combat our inner fears, eventually diverting our minds toward positivity. But, the minds of small children are like a new page that has no thoughts, mindset, or opinions of their own. Thus, it is the duty of all parents to beautifully fill in the empty pages of the manuscript with the essential skills that can stay with them forever and motivate them to keep moving ahead, even when upsetting and difficult situations pop up in their lives.

When we prepare our children for elementary school, we ensure to inculcate within them the vital qualities that could support them to succeed in their first journey of life. Instilling fundamental life skills like confidence, self-esteem, accountability, and patience acts as the key to helping your child prepare themselves for beating the odds and rising higher with beautiful colors in their life. Apart from this, practicing self-compassion, mindfulness, and setting achievable goals also help in preparing a small kid to become aware of the struggles in the current moment and contemplate feasible ideas to find an appropriate solution. This eventually develops an optimistic outlook within a small child that no door is ever made without a key. Thus, it teaches our child the basic fact that life is a mix of happiness and sorrow, success and failure, and ups and downs, but with immense courage, consistent efforts, and a positive attitude, each one of us can get over the hurdles of life and achieve success.

Promotes Self-Improvement

Self-improvement is a consistent process that must be practiced at every stage of a person's life, be it childhood, adolescence, adulthood, or beyond that. It is tricky for a person to invest in themselves and their self-improvement without prior knowledge of how to do so. Self-improvement is the ability, willingness, and capacity of an individual to work positively, effectively, and consistently toward creating a better version of themselves. Self-improvement is the efforts made to cumulatively excel in one's personal growth and also develop the pivotal qualities that help in living a better and smooth life ahead. No age barrier can restrict one from practicing this necessary life skill. However, the best time to inculcate this healthy and vital habit within oneself is childhood and parents are the foremost trainers and guides who can incline the minds and interests of the young budding soul to invest in self-improvement. The life experiences and the external environment in which a child is raised play a major role in their overall growth and development as an individual. No third person can help a child develop these skills, as self-improvement demands self-directed efforts based upon a reflection on one's abilities and limitations. In simple words, self-improvement is an umbrella term that covers endless efforts that take a child toward learning, growth, and improvement.

Many times, while preparing a child for elementary school, parents impart various academic, social, and intellectual skills to them. These skills eventually become the basis of developing the habits that push the child toward making consistent efforts, which ultimately results in self-improvement. Some of the healthy habits include practicing confidence, persistence, self-regulation, and punctuality, which surprisingly carve out their paths, making them more capable and thereby improving their core personalities. Apart from this, teaching them personal responsibility, a love of learning, personality development, practical goal setting, and an optimistic outlook cumulatively work toward their overall advancement and development. Further, the beginning of elementary school training also instills within them the spark of problem-solving, critical thinking, and decision-making, which corresponds to improving their intellectual skills. A child exhibiting such exemplary qualities can stand out among the crowd of many children, highlighting their effortless confidence, enthusiasm, eagerness, and growth mindset toward handling new and challenging tasks. Moreover, it also shows their ability to interact with their peers and make new friends easily. Thus, the act of self-improvement is good for a child's mental and physical development, as it opens the opportunity for them to participate in every task irrespective of the level of difficulty and also makes them feel good about themselves, raising their self-esteem. To accomplish this journey, initially, every child needs their parent's support, but once it becomes a part of their personality in the form of habits, they become unstoppable and fight against any negative forces, thus becoming self-sufficient enough to carry on the process of self-improvement.

Makes Child Smart and Independent

It is an overwhelming feeling for parents to imagine a time when their children become independent and self-sufficient and eventually stop needing their parents for every little thing. It is a mixed feeling for every parent because as much as we want them to grow, flourish, and stand on their own feet, at the same time, we feel left out when a child no longer needs our support to move on in life toward exploring their endeavors. Inculcating independence is one of the biggest and most precious gifts that one can present to their young budding soul as it empowers them with a strong sense that they can do and achieve anything in their life without support. Making a child independent not only assists in their growth and development but also makes them more competent and confident communicators, resilient and curious explorers, and creative thinkers. Becoming independent instills a child with a strong sense of belief that they are valued by others and that they have their own identity. Parents play a major role when it comes to making a small kid independent and smart. It is not a direct effort to make a child more independent; rather, it is a result of many indirect and simple methods that parents use to begin to teach their children to develop the qualities and habits that form a vital part of our everyday lives.

When we train a small child to go to elementary school, we make sure to make them independent enough that they are capable of eating on their own, fulfilling their potty needs, and also interacting with others to communicate if they have any issues. In the initial days, it is not easy for children to grasp the basic skills of survival, but gradually, with practice, these become a firm part of their lifestyle and identity. A small child who can manage their things on their own both at home and at school can personify their unique, smart, and independent personality. These children become an example for every other child and gain extreme appreciation and acknowledgment not only from their parents but also from their teachers. Thus, raising children with these unmatched and admirable qualities eventually adds to their confidence and boosts their self-esteem, self-motivation, and social skills. Apart from this, smart and independent children have a creative mindset, which helps them to participate in extra-curricular activities and face challenging situations. Such capable children also excel in problem-solving as they have the intellect to look into the situation from varied angles to get a feasible solution. We talk about the importance of teamwork and collaboration, but there are times when a child may be alone with no companions. In such times, an independent child would have a list of ideas that could help them entertain themselves without any help. Such is the essence of molding a child with outstanding and competent skills that not only support them in fulfilling their dreams but also help them strive for an individual and distinctive personality.

Acts as a Motivational Trigger

In this unpredictable world, we often witness various challenges of life in different forms. All these problems tend to make us vulnerable and expose us to harsh negativities that drive us to give up on our tasks, lowering our morale and enthusiasm to live life. As it is truly said, things learned in childhood always form an intact part of our memory and keep reminding us of the happenings of the past, either positively or negatively, depending on the lessons learned. Thus, it is important to create such motivating memories in our children's lives that can push them forward in times of trials, helping them to win over all the negative emotions and situations. While in the process of training and equipping the child with basic life skills, there are times when our child falls down or experiences failure in a task. At such a delicate moment, they look at us for what to do in the hope of getting the best guidance to achieve their dreams and aspirations, which seem to be running out of their hands.

In any such situation, we should never underestimate our children. Instead, we should motivate them to rise again with full courage and confidence to bag their goals. In the same way, when our little ones start their elementary schooling, they often make mistakes in their academics, become victims of bullying by their peers, or even face criticism from their teachers. All these scenarios tend to demoralize the child by questioning their creativity and capability to interact and make good friends. But, when children have received proper training before getting enrolled in elementary school, they recall the lessons of positivity, courage, confidence, and willpower that was taught to them by their parents whenever they failed at doing something at home. These teachings imparted to the child at their sensitive age act as the motivational trigger that inspires them to stand strong against all the odds and mark their victory as successful learners.

Chapter 6:

Simple Methods to Teach

Your Child With Ease

Tell me and I forget. Teach me and I remember. Involve me and I learn. —Benjamin Franklin, an American Polymath

With fast-paced, growing technology, the world is changing dramatically, and so are the minds of young little souls. Imagine yourself using a traditional analog phone in the era of smartphones or cooking meals using an earth oven instead of the modern kitchen range. Not only would using these older techniques create many problems for you, but it would also be time-consuming, less effective, inefficient, and boring. Similar to the way we choose the best technologies and advanced methods for our convenience, it is important to consider innovative and creative ways of imparting education to these small children.

The traditional and outdated ways of teaching only focused on inculcating the academic skills that could support a child to improve their performance and achieve better grades. However, things have changed globally due to rising competition and the endeavor to develop distinctive and outstanding skills that can help one to add a jewel to their crown. Elementary schooling is the stepping stone for instilling magnificent skills and characteristics within a child that not only boost their academic performance but also support them in becoming the finest version of themselves to keep themselves motivated and ace it in their later life. Therefore, it is an urgent need of the hour for parents and teachers to reflect on and rethink the techniques they are implementing to provide education to children. We must strive toward raising a child with distinguished qualities that can help them shine brighter among the crowd and carve their path toward success, and this can only be done through using the best and most effective teaching methods. So, let's contemplate and summarize the popular, creative, and innovative strategies that can thrill and engage children throughout the learning process and fill their minds with strength, courage, and determination to adapt and face every challenging task with great enthusiasm.

Activity-Based Teaching

Raising a successful child is not about piling them up with loads of books that must be learned by heart to pass an exam and achieve perfect results. Rather, an effective learning and teaching approach is about inculcating the right skills and apt knowledge along with emotional and social lessons. Activity-based learning is gaining a huge awareness and demand among teachers, parents, and students as it is the basis to involve a child mentally as well physically in the activities that provide them with an efficient learning experience. Activity-based learning, also called learning by doing, is a psychological approach to teaching children where a child is directly allowed to participate in the process of learning rather than sitting as a passive listener in a classroom. Activity-based learning provides a platform where a small kid is guided through instruction by a teacher or parent to perform varied tasks and activities, independently investigate and problem-solve, and conduct experiments. Learning by doing is a special approach that provides the leverage to a child to completely engage in the process, which allows them to choose the best tools that work for them.

Activity-based learning has many benefits for elementary school students as it provides an innovative learning experience that boosts their creativity, critical analysis, problem-solving, imaginary powers, and reasoning skills and gives them a platform where they can express their thinking and knowledge (Acharyya, 2021). Learning by doing is one of the best teaching methods that inculcates confidence, team building, and cohesion, enriches vocabulary, develops keen interest, and also acts as a stimulus for reading and learning. Therefore, providing an optimum learning environment to small children opens the opportunity for them to explore and do various activities on their own, which develops a huge sense of inspiration for learning and helps them retain the information for longer.

Value-Based Teaching

In today's modern world, every parent is keen on providing the best education to their children, which is not only confined to extracting bookish knowledge and information but rather covers the aspects beyond that. To face the challenges and succeed in a globally competitive world, parents must opt for a teaching method that helps in the overall development of a child and not one that is limited to performing well in academics alone. One such fascinating yet effective method of teaching is value-based education. Value-based education supports a child to make the appropriate decision whenever they are stuck in the dilemma of choosing the right path for their goals, which work wonders for them even when they group up into an adult. Value-based education lays the foundation for the core development of a child, which not only shapes their career but also enlightens their personality with exquisite morals and values (Gupta, 2023). In this learning approach, the teacher emphasizes teaching the values to the students in a classroom through textbooks, role-plays, and live examples outside school. The main notion behind instilling values within children is to foster more peace, tolerance, and understanding of diverse cultural, political, and religious variations.

Imparting values through value-based education cultivates significant characteristics within children, like compassion, kindness, and empathy, which are the basis for teaching them better social and emotional skills. Furthermore, moral values are fundamental in that they enhance decision-making capabilities and support a child to make the right decision in any difficult situation. Value-based learning helps children to evolve in a positive direction, which gives them a better sense of responsibility and understanding of their purpose in life. Therefore, value-based learning is the key that induces small kids to perform positive and acceptable behaviors, which develops not only intelligence but also the right set of values that prepare them for any challenging life situation when they grow up.

Technology-Based Teaching

The new generation of kids, often referred to as Generation Alpha, are known to be born with unique excellence, smartness, and intelligence as they are already a tech-savvy peer group who are hands-on using the new technology. In the current era, it is not an uncommon sight to find a small child holding a mobile phone or tablet or trying to use a laptop, which not only proves that they are eager to use this technology but are surprisingly capable. In this technologically advanced world, it is unfair if parents and teachers do not reflect on the ability of technology to provide an enhanced and meaningful learning experience to kids. Technology-based learning, as the name implies, is a teaching style that utilizes the wide range of technology available to make the journey of learning smoother and hurdle-free for small children. There are several ways to integrate technology within the classroom and even at home to improve the learning process, for instance, using virtual classrooms, laptops, tablets, PowerPoint presentations, projectors, online grading systems, or online homework and assignments. Apart from this, there are many other applications like Nearpod, which help in creating an interactive and intriguing session for engaging more children in the process of learning (Simpson, 2021).

The use of technology for imparting proper learning to elementary school children serves amazing benefits, like helping to make concepts clearer by engaging children and supporting the retention of information for longer. The best part about this learning approach is that it can used to support any type of learning style, for instance, visual, auditory, or tactile, also known as kinesthetic, based upon what style suits the child. Using technology for learning also makes it quite easy and possible for students to share information or notes among friends, which enhances their social skills and teamwork capabilities. Therefore, choosing a technology-based approach not only boosts academic performance but also prepares a child for the future by making them more familiar and comfortable with the different technologies.

Peer Interaction-Based Teaching

As parents, we are always on the hunt for a feasible method that can support a five-year-old to actively participate in the learning process. However, learning can be a daunting task for an elementary school child because of the anxiety and fear developed due to leaving parents and staying away for hours at a new place. When a kid's mind is preoccupied with such upsetting thoughts, confusion, and stress, it becomes challenging for them to concentrate on the learning process. One beneficial technique that supports an effective learning process within small children is peer interaction-based learning. Peer-to-peer learning, as the name indicates, is a method that promotes collaboration between different students within a classroom to learn, support other kids, and participate in problem-solving and understanding of concepts (Drew, 2019). It is two-way learning that creates a comfortable, intriguing, and productive atmosphere, which is the best for learning. There are many ways through which a teacher can support peer interaction-based learning, for instance, by creating small groups of children who interact with each other and work together to solve problems or present a certain topic in the classroom. Teachers can also promote activities like debates, group discussions, and elocution among the children to improve peer interaction and impart information.

Peer interaction-based learning is an extraordinary teaching method that not only benefits small children by increasing their interest and participation in active learning, but it also inculcates the right qualities in children that can help them succeed in later life. For instance, peer-to-peer interaction enhances the team working skills, boosts effective communication, and encourages healthy competition among kids. With this learning technique, children can get honest feedback by recognizing gaps within their extracted information. Peer interaction supports a child to get out of their shy and reserved zone, which gradually builds confidence and enhances their self-esteem. Thus, apart from serving the benefits of providing a healthy learning environment, peer-to-peer learning also adds more fun to the entire process of learning.

Project-Based Teaching

The traditional teaching methods that are focused on imparting education only through face-to-face interaction between a teacher and their students do not involve any kind of new or innovative techniques. In such teaching settings, it becomes quite challenging for teachers to inculcate the basics as most children fail to understand the concepts, which shows up in their low grades and reduced performances. To improve teaching effectiveness in the classroom, teachers need to opt for creative and diverse ways that can support children to learn faster. Project-based learning is one such technique, as it emphasizes giving the authority and freedom to children to explore real-life problems, which guides them toward a deeper understanding of the concepts. The main idea behind project-based learning is to divide the children into groups of four to six students while assigning them a tricky time-based project to investigate the questions and complicated problems (Sitwell, 2021). To successfully implement project-based learning among children, teachers must focus on deciding which projects have a good purpose and will catch the attention of the group of students based on their level of understanding, knowledge, and skills. It is important to choose projects with case issues and also inspire children to work on projects of their choice by creating something interesting to boost their learning experience. Some of the best project-based ideas for elementary school kids are to compose, examine, and explain a self-written poem, encourage them to solve an environmental problem, or ask them to decide on a career of their choice and explore the basic requirements to achieving that career.

Project-based learning is a remarkable teaching approach that not only provides amazing benefits to children but also opens up endless opportunities to grow and flourish through learning. Deciding to take up a project develops confidence within kids to boldly face any challenge without fearing failure. As projects are always done in groups, it teaches teamwork and collaboration to these young souls, which not only improves their social skills but also helps them adopt healthy habits for a lifetime. Thus, the project-based teaching method is the best one for engaging a student to a great extent and helps to broaden the spectrum of their understanding ability, develops interest, and makes them feel connected to the learning process.

Chapter 7:

Tips to Help Your Child

Become a Quick Learner

A child must know that he is a miracle, that since the beginning of the world, there hasn't been, and until the end of the world, there will not be, another child like him. —Pablo Casals, a Spanish Musician

A child is born with an innate characteristic of being curious and eager to explore the world around them and soak up all the new and interesting skills and information within them like a sponge. However, as a child begins to grow up, their enthusiasm and natural love to get the answer about everything that is going on around them is lost somewhere. Many big and small reasons impact the willingness of a kid to engage in learning activities, like demotivation, peer competition and pressure, excessive lectures and lack of support from parents, a feeling of low self-esteem, and poor self-confidence. Not every good student is born a good learner; rather, the skill of learning is something that can be inculcated in a small child at any time. The most important ingredients that boost learning skills in young children are the right motivation, external support, a suitable atmosphere, healthy habits, and a positive outlook toward challenging situations.

However, one of the biggest mistakes that most parents and teachers make is keeping the act of learning limited only within the four walls of the school. Learning is not only the ability of a child to understand and gain knowledge about the core subjects taught in a school. It is also a continuous process that entails observations, logical questioning, critical thinking, and developing perspectives. No doubt, a classroom is the primary place where a child starts to learn, but this process must be continued at home, when they are out with family and friends, or while playing games and other activities. Therefore, it is important to know the basic tips and tricks that can support a parent to provide the right guidance to their child that inculcates learning within them. So, let's uncover and get familiar with the key life hacks that are the life savior for a small child and induce better learning skills to enlighten their present as well as future.

Start Slow

Training a small child to inculcate basic learning skills is not a simple task that can be done overnight by simply flicking a magical wand. Rather, it is a phenomenon that requires an abundance of patience, practice, perseverance, and plenty of time. Teaching learning skills to a five-year-old is considered a tricky quest by most parents, as it requires a child to develop many qualities at the same time, like recognizing, understanding, following instructions, writing, reading, and many more. However, burdening small kids by pressuring them to learn so many skills simultaneously could be intimidating, stressful, and irritating for them. Such wrong and negative gestures of a parent to make their child learn can have an inverse impact on their mind and learning capabilities and can cause them to run away from the entire process. Thus, to avoid these unwanted and unhealthy reactions by children, parents should begin slowly by teaching one skill at a moment. Starting slowly not only helps the child feel relaxed and comfortable but also brushes up their skills enough that they can grasp the concepts better, which builds a strong foundation for their later educational life.

Break the Process Into Simple Steps

Inculcating the right learning skills in a small kid can become an exhausting job for parents if they fail to understand the nature, thought process, capabilities, interests, and problems associated with them. The learning process can also become a challenging one for young children if they are not provided with the required appropriate guidance by their parents. As every child has a vast difference in their attitudes and grasping abilities, the approach, tips, and tricks that parents use must also be different. Therefore, parents must invest enough time to unveil the techniques that best suit their children and boost their learning skills. Every child faces some or the other different issues that can impact their learning abilities, like physical fitness, memory, anxiety, fear, delayed fine motor skills, and poor understanding of the basics. Therefore, breaking the entire process into smaller segments is a feasible option that helps a parent impart the proper training and instill learning skills within their child. Step-by-step training also supports and ensures that a child develops an interest in and enthusiasm for the learning process. For instance, you can start by making the child familiar with the syllabus, gradually shift to recognizing the alphabet and numbers and saying them out loud, then move on to writing, and so on.

Focus on Their Strengths

Every child is unique as they are born with different talents, strengths, and capabilities. However, just as each one of us has weak points, small children also have weaknesses that may restrict them from performing their best in academics. As a parent is a foremost guide and moral support for a small child, it is very important for them to highlight and work on the strengths of their kid rather than only focusing on the flaws, as it only worsens their abilities and morale to try new things. The more you talk about what a child cannot do, the more they fall apart from within. It weakens and discourages them, becomes the reason for their distress, and steals away their enthusiasm and desire to learn. However, when a parent focuses on their kid's strengths, it boosts their motivation, mental and emotional health, and eagerness to try difficult things, eventually raising their learning capabilities and improving their school performance. For instance, when your child fails in English, instead of yelling and punishing them for their results, try to focus on the subjects in which they performed better and achieved good marks by appreciating them and congratulating them for their efforts. Developing this attitude would encourage a child to self-analyze their weak points and work hard in other subjects to improve their overall performance.

Don't Over Expect From Them

The main motive behind inculcating learning skills within small children is to make them understand the basic concepts and improve their critical thinking, which eventually boosts their academic performance and grades in school. However, many a time, parents fail to understand the rationale behind sending a child to school. They often develop a perception that improved learning means higher grades and excellence in academic performance. Gradually, parents build up higher expectations of their children, which creates undue pressure and stress in the minds of these young kids. Eventually, a small child starts feeling it as a compulsion to bring good marks on a test, whether or not they have the required skills and capabilities to do so, which impacts their morale, learning abilities, and concentration at school. Instead, parents must make it a point to focus on what a child is learning daily and not on how they are performing at school. Sometimes, a child who is a good learner fails to convert it into good grades due to many reasons like lack of time, health issues, distraction, or anxiety and fear. Therefore, having over expectations and being judgmental about the learning skills of a child based upon their performance could only reduce their motivation and degrade their performance further.

Give Them Time to Learn

As soon as a child enters elementary school, most parents start putting efforts to push their children toward learning. However, we often fail to realize that there is no magical spell that makes a child learn within hours. Rather, learning is a continuous process that happens over time when done with consistency and the right efforts. Develop a practice to make a child learn every day without fail by asking them questions while they are playing or when you are spending time with the family on a trip, as it helps them grasp the lessons faster. Also, make it a habit to discuss the different subjects your child studies with them and help them better understand the concepts they have learned by asking them to classify, categorize, and practice critical thinking about what they see and experience in real life. Adopting such techniques supports a parent to inculcate a healthy habit of learning within a child, which internally motivates them and improves their concentration in the classroom and even at home. Learning is a life-changing skill that, once developed in a small child, can direct them in the correct and progressive direction as they grow up.

Appreciate Their Small Achievements

Parents can't force a habit of learning onto their children. Rather, using diverse and effective ways like rewards, appreciation, and acknowledgment are the hacks that help in doing the needful. Learning is an all-new and difficult process for young kids, which may take immense time for them to gain perfection. Every time your child puts in an effort that shows a positive result, make it a point to appreciate them. You can acknowledge your child's hard work by either using an emotional method like appreciation or spending some precious time with them, or the reward method by buying them chocolates or toys. However, a parent must be mindful that the gesture of rewarding them is not misinterpreted as a bribe because it would have a drastic reverse impact on their mind, eventually reducing the effectiveness of the process. Further, parents must also be careful not to praise mediocrity as that would dramatically change their behavior toward adapting to the process of learning. However, celebrating and recognizing the achievements of a small child empowers them with the strength to perform better next time, as it provides them with the encouragement to try again even after a failure.

Make the Learning Process a Fun-Filled Journey

Starting an elementary school loads a child with lots of new responsibilities, challenging tasks, and assignments. These things can scare a kid and have a strong negative impact on their innocent mind, which can divert their minds, thus affecting their overall academic performance. Learning is an important phase of life as it helps a child to grow and prosper, eventually leading them toward success and development. Therefore, it is necessary to adopt techniques that can both mentally and physically support a child to enthusiastically participate in the learning process. One such fun way of learning is game-based learning, which is not a new concept and serves numerous benefits like providing an opportunity for deep learning and also brushing their non-cognitive skills. Games can be in any form, be it online video games, outdoor sports, playful events, or indoor educational games. Playing such types of games helps drive a child's interest and eagerness to explore, understand, and learn new things. Apart from this, games also add entertainment to the entire learning process, which intrigues their attention, provides pleasure, and engages them in learning. Sometimes, when a game is played in a group with other children, it teaches them the skill of teamwork, which is a crucial requirement for children going to elementary school.

Replace Lectures with Healthy Discussions

One of the biggest mistakes that most parents make when trying to promote learning in small children is to start giving them unwanted and lengthy lectures. We forget that the mind of a small child is too immature to understand the worldly and big talks about success, manners, habits, and learning. Repeatedly giving lectures and yelling at them can induce unwanted fear within them. Sometimes, such gestures can also embed feelings of inferiority and low self-esteem that gradually occupy a larger space in their mind. A small child with such negative thoughts and perceptions about themselves can never succeed in the process of learning. Instead, the fear of failure and the pressure of parents could degrade their capabilities, eventually leading to poor academic performance. Therefore, one must always be mindful while talking to a small kid and replace lectures with healthy discussions. When you make it a habit to discuss the good things and the problems of children, it empowers them with the courage to ask questions and to share their problems without the concern of being judged, condemned, or humiliated. Parents who practice active listening and indulge in two-way conversations with their children strengthen them with the confidence, authority, and right to seek help without a second thought, which is important for learning.

Become Their Support System

Our perception of a thing largely impacts the actions that we perform in reaction to the situation. Similarly, in the case of small children, when learning becomes a problematic and difficult task that burdens a child with stress and pressure, it is obvious that they would never be able to succeed in that endeavor. Building a small child's perception is completely in the hands of their parents, as they are their foremost support system. When parents encourage a child with motivating words and make them feel that taking up challenges aids in boosting their learning capabilities, they are more likely to strategize, prioritize, and work hard toward getting an appropriate solution to the problem. However, a child who believes that learning and gaining excellence in academics is only meant for intelligent students can be expected to run away from problems and avoid facing any fears because of the concern of failure. Therefore, parents must motivate, support, and understand their kids when they fail, rather than showing anger or frustration as it would, in turn, affect their capabilities, interest, and morale. Making them believe that learning is a simple process that has nothing to do with perfection or achievement eventually builds up more enthusiasm and eagerness in a child to engage in the learning process.

Develop a Habit of Reading

For some people, reading is a form of entertainment that helps their mind relax and improves the imaginary and creative power of their brain. While reading is an important art, for young children, it is considered the key to strengthening their learning skills. When parents support their children in developing a love of reading, it automatically increases their love for learning, while children who face difficulty in reading eventually face severe challenges during learning. Thus, reading lays the foundation for learning as it not only boosts formal communication and the ability of the brain to process the concepts but also improves their vocabulary. Polished reading skills extend the abilities of small children far beyond improving their language skills; they also enhance their learning skills for different subjects like math. Parents must focus on developing their children's reading habits from a very young age by creating an atmosphere at home where each family member indulges in some type of reading for at least 15 to 20 minutes. Apart from this, taking your five-year-old along with you to choose a book of their choice can develop their interest and enthusiasm to participate in the act of reading, which eventually boosts their learning capabilities.

Figure Out Your Child's Learning Style

More than the efforts that parents put in to make their children learn, the approach that they follow to induce this skill is what makes the change. No two children are the same, be it their physical stamina, emotional status, or mental strength; therefore, their ability to grasp and learn also varies from each other. When a parent has the appropriate idea about the learning style that would suit their child the most, it eases the entire process by making it most effective for them. Researchers have identified three basic learning styles: auditory, visual, and kinesthetic (Cullins, 2022b). The auditory learning method emphasizes the hearing and listening qualities of a learner, as they are good listeners who can easily follow instructions and have musical aptitude and verbal strength. In the visual learning technique, the learner can process the details and knowledge in the form of images or writing as they are the ones who enjoy art, have a sharp and excellent memory, and are keenly observant. The kinesthetic learning method is used for learners who are good in physical activities and sports, as they grasp the information based on physical touch, using hand gestures, or counting on fingers. You can easily decide the learning approach that would best suit your child by answering the questions available on an online assessment portal. However, it is also possible for you to investigate the best type of learning style based on your child's interests, habits, likes and dislikes, and the type of games and activities they enjoy. Therefore, the key to teaching a child apt learning skills is to identify their strengths and trigger points that stimulate fast learning and understanding of the concepts.

Chapter 8:

Qualities a Parent Must Have to Train Their Children

Don't worry that children never listen to you; worry that they are always watching you. —Robert Fulghum, an American Writer

In this highly advanced and fast-paced world, every parent aspires to raise a child who has strong competitive skills that can support them to establish their footing in the crowds of millions of talented children. Childhood is a crucial stage in a person's life as it lays the solid foundation for a small kid to grow up into a mature adult who has all the necessary skills that can help them succeed in life. However, we often ignore that the qualities of parents and their parenting style have a lot of influence when it comes to imparting the suitable and most wanted skills to small children. As they say, a child is the best reflection of their parents; therefore, a parent must portray an earnest and exemplary way of doing things as it guides their children to follow in the same footsteps and rise higher in their lives.

Parenting is not only about helping kids learn and grow; rather, it is a broad concept that encompasses multiple aspects of a parent's and child's life together. Good parenting requires certain qualities that accumulate in the actions and interactions parents have with their children and is driven by determined goals and purposes in mind. Developing strong parental skills helps in making a child more adjustable, eventually boosting their mental, physical, and emotional well-being. With better parental skills, parents can improve their relationship with a child as they feel more connected and secure, which makes them value the parent's input and trust them. When a child feels confident, safe, heard, and understood by their parents, they feel easy and comfortable approaching them for their needs, concerns, and problems in every phase of life. But, as every parent is not perfect, there is always a scope to improve oneself, correct, and learn the basic parental skills that can support a small child to enter their new phase of life with ease, excitement, and enthusiasm. So, let's have a quick look at the simple yet strong, spirited, and significant skills that are the heart and soul of parenting style, which must be adopted by every parent to train them with the right qualities.

Patience

Just as nourishment and food are necessary for survival, patience is the most necessary quality for successful parenting. For a parent, patience is not just a virtue; rather, it is an imperative need, without which it is not easy for them to maintain a healthy parent-child relationship. However, many parents struggle with innumerable issues while dealing with their children, which is mostly due to their inability to practice patience. Every parent aspires to teach good manners and healthy habits to their child, but doing so without patience can be challenging and stressful.

Life is not always as we expect it to be, as many times, a challenging situation pops up when we simply want to make a child ready to go to school. However, yelling and nagging them at this young age is not justified as they are too small to understand these gestures. Thus, as parents, we need to calm down and maintain our patience to deal with these young budding souls. A small child is not capable or mature enough to take lessons from their parents' anger and frustrations. As children learn what they see, it is very important to be a role model for them by exhibiting good qualities like patience. To boost our patience, we can try to repeat positive affirmations, practice meditation, and take care of our personal and emotional needs to enhance this crucial skill and keep our emotions in control.

Tolerance

Parents not only have the responsibility to raise their children with acceptable manners and justified behaviors, but they are the ones who must provide the best life for them, which requires extensive efforts and struggles. Busy in the hustle and bustle of securing the best for their children, it is obvious why parents may lose their temper when their young children exhibit unacceptable behaviors. However, using such strict methods of discipline, like harsh verbal reprimands or even hitting, has never worked for parents as they only make a child defiant, stubborn, and more likely to repeat these behaviors. Showing tolerance in such situations and correcting them later on makes them realize their mistakes and helps shape the desired behavior, which helps in improved learning and teaches them tolerance as well.

Tolerance is the ability and willingness of a parent to bear the behaviors of their child that they do not necessarily agree with. Every child is unique, but they share a common point when it comes to doing mischievous and intolerable activities. However, the best way to deal with these innocent minds is to show tolerance based upon the situation to correct them and convince them to avoid doing the same again. Thus, tolerance is an exquisite tool in the parental tool kit to raise happy and healthy children, as it gives them some space to realize their mistakes and learn from them.

Compassion

For most children, the idea of going to an elementary school for the very first time and staying away from parents and home is quite stressful and draining. Due to this pressure, a child sometimes feels unable to express their emotions and may begin to behave irritably and aggressively. If parents are unable to understand the unsaid words of what their child is going through, it creates a distance between them and may become the reason for a child's increased negative behavior. The best way to handle such circumstances is to have compassion for those little innocent souls. As small children are in much need of parental support and compassion, we, as parents, must understand the pressure on them and must put in the effort to make them feel relaxed and normal.

Compassion is the quality that helps parents to step into the shoes of their young children and become aware of what they are going through. Compassion is not only important when a child enters the stage of going to school; instead, it is the backbone of the parent-child relationship. Be it teaching good manners or simply meeting the physical and emotional needs of a child, we can show them the right path toward achieving their goals and dreams very easily by simply exhibiting unconditional love, kindness, and compassion toward our growing children.

Anger Management

Anger is a normal and natural human emotion that happens to each one of us. Sometimes, anger is perceived as a positive emotion as it empowers us with the strength and fire to achieve our goals. However, the same anger can become a wrong and harmful emotion when a parent vents at a small child. Whether or not a child has made a mistake, dealing with a situation by exhibiting anger never leads to positive solutions. Parents have a great responsibility on their shoulders to raise a child with the right skills that become the lifeline to establish their strong position and achieve success in this world. However, being involved in other demanding tasks like balancing home, work life, social activities, children's time, and household chores may often result in feeling angry. Sometimes, a relationship issue with a partner, the annoying and frustrating behaviors of children, or financial issues can also become the reason for losing one's temper.

Whatever the reason, showing anger to a small child is never good as it drastically impacts their mind and sometimes even affects their mental and emotional growth, leading to other problems, like depression, anxiety, disinterest in studies, or lack of concentration. Therefore, one must be mindful as a parent and focus on practicing anger management. Some of the best anger management tricks for parents are to reflect on the cause of anger, look for tips to calm down, or practice meditation to let go of the negativities from within.

Time Management

Apart from the above-mentioned parenting skills, a parent must excel in time management if they are looking forward to training their child with the best qualities. Parents juggle to get things done on time, especially if they have toddlers and small children. However, there are days when getting everything done at the right time becomes a challenging task, making one feel stressed and leaving behind a preoccupied mind. Feeling the pressure of time management is natural with every parent, but getting over these draining emotions and starting fresh another day is what keeps you going. Parents who struggle with managing household chores, professional deadlines, personal life goals, and supporting kids must focus on improving their time management skills.

Most of the time, when parents are bad at managing their everyday schedule, they often compromise with their children, which results in a guilt trip as you feel that you are doing wrong by not giving the time and attention. To compensate for this feeling, many parents send their kids off to be engaged in extra-curricular activities with the aim that they will learn new skills. However, doing so only creates a rift in the parent-child relationship and makes it difficult for a child to connect with their parents. Thus, time management is a significant part of parenting as spending time with your child can help in educating them on humility, etiquette, and good character, which can only happen if they develop a strong bond with their family. Therefore, once you have mastered the skill of time management, you can easily spare some precious time in your day to invest in training your child in the right skills. Some of the simple ways to manage time properly are by prioritizing the important tasks, sticking to a proper routine, delegating extra important tasks to other people that need not be necessarily done by you, having a menu plan for every week, and many more.

Positive Mindset

As parents, it is necessary for us to analyze and understand the mindset of our children by exploring whether they perceive half a glass of water as half-full or half-empty, which defines their approach to life and its challenges. In parenting, it matters what thought process you have at the back of your mind for most time of the day. Imagine yourself being frustrated, annoyed, and having a negative perception of everything that is going on around you. In such a situation, it becomes challenging for you to avoid venting your emotions to your little kids, who often do mischievous activities. When you have a negative mindset, everything that comes and goes around you will bother you to infinity, eventually giving rise to empty threats, exaggerating the scenarios, overreacting, yelling, and, in the worst case, hitting the child. Instead, developing a positive mindset can help you to handle situations more calmly and practically, which is the basis for enhancing your parenting style.

Remember, a child's mind is greatly impacted by what their parent does, thinks, and how they behave. If you begin to practice a positive mindset, it will be inculcated into your child, which is the most crucial factor for uplifting their thought process, boosting happiness, and improving overall well-being. A positive mindset is a key trait that helps parents to educate their children, solve their problems, support them in school and extracurricular activities, understand their concerns and problems, and guide them toward having an optimistic outlook about every obstacle coming in the path of their life. Therefore, parents must invest in developing a positive mindset by practicing positive affirmations, doing meditation, keeping their expectations low from a child, connecting with their child instead of criticizing them, and transforming their perceptions negatively.

Chapter 9:

Myths About Training a Child Before Elementary School

If we don't shape our kids, they will be shaped by outside forces that don't care what shape our kids are in. —Dr. Louise Hart, the Best Selling Author

Handling and entertaining young budding children who are full of enthusiasm and energy to explore the whole world around them is definitely an arduous task. As parents, we are endowed with the crucial responsibility to nourish, train, and educate our little angels in their initial learning age in order to make them independent, active, and successful in their lives. However, in an attempt to provide our kids with all the goodness and knowledge of basic survival skills, we often fall prey to various hypothetical fallacies which tend to mislead us. However, the fact is that many of the commonly believed myths are just the outcome of the exceptional thinking of a few ignorant parents who have created negative opinions regarding bringing up and training young children before enrolling them in elementary schools.

Thus, as parents, it is our prime duty to explore and understand each and every aspect of different said and heard things that hover around our children to guard them against any unwanted diversions in their lives. So, let's quickly uncover and debunk a number of misinterpreted thoughts and beliefs that may hinder a child from learning and performing their best.

Pre-Schooling is the Same as Babysitting

Many times, it may happen that due to some unfavorable reasons like some health issues or other distractions, parents may not be able to focus on their child's early development and thus do not contribute effectively to teaching them the ABCs of life skills. In such cases, many parents opt to enroll their little ones in preschools and Montessori schools in order to support their proper development and learning phase with the help of special teachers. The main aim of preschooling is to equip the child with all the basic skills and talents that would be of great help to them once they get enrolled in elementary schools. One of the most ridiculous things that you might have heard while preschooling your child is that some people refer to preschooling as merely an act of babysitting. However, the fact is far different from this fallacy, as in babysitting, the person taking care of the child basically focuses on comforting the child in the absence of their parents, unlike preschooling, where the early childhood educator aims to prepare the child for a bright future and successful life. Thus, children who are trained in preschools become fully prepared with the fundamental academic skills, motor skills, and social skills, along with a higher level of emotional and psychological stability that can ease their journey toward elementary schooling by assisting them at each and every step.

No Special Teaching is Required Before Elementary Schooling

Every child is born special, as each one of them has different capabilities, thought processes, and learning abilities, which makes them unique in their own way. Many children often tend to learn very quickly and efficiently just by observing and grasping the things happening around them. However, there are children who need time to understand and learn what is being taught to them in their daily life. In today's modern world, there are many busy parents who believe that children don't need to be trained or equipped with any special skills before joining their first school, as they will learn everything once they go to school. This rigid misbelief of parents hinders the child from acquiring basic survival skills that are necessary for them to cope in the environment of elementary schools, which demands the child to be independent enough to eat, drink, read, write, and even attend nature's call by themselves. Thus, it is important for every parent to understand and respond according to the needs and capabilities of their child instead of going with the crowd and developing such a mindset that will eventually trim their wings off, even before they have taken their first flight in life. So, as parents, we should help and guide our children in order to make them smart, self-dependent, and confident enough to face the world with pride and enthusiasm.

Too Much Strictness Can Help in Better Training

It is true that managing and training little naughty kids is a great, challenging task, as these small packets of energy and enthusiasm are always up to some or the other unexpected and innovative activity. In this sensitive growing age, kids encounter many new things in their life that raises numerous questions in their young minds. Thus, to find the apt answers to these queries, children approach their most trusted source—their parents. However, many busy and working parents often find it annoying and disturbing to handle all these kinds of things, as they are already preoccupied with various tensions, work priorities, and lack of time. All this compels them to believe that being strict with their little ones can discipline them and avoid any such mess and tantrums created by them. However, in the haze of life's race, we overlook the fact that children are blessed with an inquisitive attitude that drives them to explore and ask questions, which eventually contributes to their positive development. Thus, by adopting harsh and unkind attitudes toward our children, we are teaching them the wrong way of behaving with others. Moreover, it will create fear and hesitation in the minds of young children, which will eventually confine them, restricting their interaction and hindering their growth as an individual.

Playing Cannot Be a Way of Teaching Young Children

In this competitive world, all parents want their children to shine bright like a star in all aspects of their life. To achieve this, they put all their efforts into helping their children learn and grasp different skills and excel in various activities. However, in a haze to focus on their child's development, many times parents start believing that their child is wasting time by playing and thus impose restrictions on them, confining them to books and preschool alone. While doing so, they don't realize that this act of strictness can harm their growing inquisitiveness and positive mindset. Childhood is a tender age, and most kids love to explore differently by playing and interacting with the things and people around them. In fact, playing is one of the easiest ways to equip the child with various academic and social skills like counting numbers, identifying objects, differentiating colors, understanding relationships, etc. Thus, as parents, we must understand the simple ways by which we can boost our children's efficiency in learning and encourage them to expand the ocean of their knowledge by diving deep into their world of imagination and exploring the hidden aspects of life.

Training a Young Child is an Easy Task

Children are the greatest gift of the Divine to every parent. They are precious enough that we put in great effort to provide them with the best of everything in this world, be it nutritious food, a healthy lifestyle, good habits, favorite toys, or simply the best learning process. We all eagerly want to teach our children, polish their skills, and inculcate the right learning habits in them. However, dealing with a young child may sometimes get on our nerves, but that is not what makes it a daunting task. Parents sometimes feel anxious and stressed out while training their small children, which can be due to many possible reasons like the pressure of societal norms about learning, a child's academic performance and grades, and many more such things. Nowadays, in many families, both parents are occupied with the professional burden, making it quite tricky for them to maintain a work-life balance and invest some precious time with their little one, which is the foremost requirement for training them. Further, in this high-tech world, every parent is keen to gain much information about parenting hacks that can help them make things easy and effective for them. This can lead many parents to overload themselves with too much information that often gets mixed up and creates confusion about what style is best suited for their child and can train them effectively. Therefore, training has become difficult for parents due to external governing factors, the blame and burden of which is often levied on the shoulders of small children.

Training Kids Before Elementary Schooling Overburdens Them

Many times in life, during the process of preparing our children for starting their early elementary education, we come across the most commonly heard myth that the act of training the child before sending them to school overburdens them. In today's competitive world, every parent wishes to see their child reach the heights of success by achieving their dreams right from a young age. Thus, the majority of parents opt for equipping their children with the necessary academic, social, and physical skills that mark the beginning of the journey toward learning. However, there are parents who are inspired by the old-fashioned thoughts of people who think and believe in the fallacy that young children have limited skills and capabilities, which develop only when they grow older. But, the fact is entirely different from this, as the more we expose our children to the surrounding world and daily activities, the more they get interested and the faster they learn. Thus, as parents, it is our duty to understand and decide wisely what will be the best choice for our child rather than being influenced by what other people say around us.

Conclusion

Ready, Steady, Go to School is an interesting guide that aims to highlight the benefits and importance of preparing and training little children before sending them to elementary schools. The book beautifully explains the journey of understanding the mindset of young children and their abilities by exploring the challenges and difficulties that may come on their way toward efficient learning of basic life skills. Moreover, the book also discusses the barriers that may hinder parents from giving their best in the course of guiding their little ones toward a bright and independent future. The book is a perfect read for all those parents who aspire to make their children self-dependent, responsible, and confident by adopting different interesting ways of teaching them using advanced educational approaches, which will surely bring about a positive change in both their lives.

The book also focuses on providing essential tips and hacks, along with emphasizing the vital traits that a parent must possess in order to assist their child in grasping and learning things at a faster pace, thus making the little ones jacks of all trades. In the endeavor to create awareness among parents, the book encloses a fun-filled section that engages all parents by debunking the most commonly heard and believed myths and fallacies that surround the concept of training a child before elementary school. Overall, the book's main purpose is to make the whole process of learning and teaching for both budding young kids and enthusiastic parents a memorable and enjoyable one.

Lastly, I would wholeheartedly thank all my passionate readers who made great efforts to spare their precious time to read this book, which focuses on providing a new vision to all the parents out there aiming to give a good start to their children in their lives. I am glad to share with you that I am very eager to read your reviews on the book, as your feedback is very valuable to me and has the capability to motivate and guide me to create more interesting books like this in the future. By now, your minds would be occupied by a turmoil of several intriguing questions that may be making you impatient and compelling you to find answers to them. So, let's try to discover and embrace a new and engaging concept to raise children with these heart-searching questions:

- How should I prepare my child for learning new skills?

- Can preparing my child before elementary school make the journey toward learning easier?

- How should I select the best teaching technique for my child?

- How do I understand my child is interested in the learning process?

- Can other family members assist my child in the journey of learning before starting elementary schooling?

- How can I make my child more skilled, confident, and independent in terms of essential life skills?

References

Acharyya, A. (2021, August 31). *Benefits of activity-based learning.* Vawsum. https://vawsum.com/benefits-of-activity-based-learning-for-students/

Alexander, L. (2023, March 21). *How to teach respect to kids (5 Ways to Do It).* Mom Loves Best. https://momlovesbest.com/how-to-teach-respect-to-kids

Chopra, D. (2021, January 18). *How to determine the best age to start kindergarten.* Orchids. https://www.orchidsinternationalschool.com/blog/parents-corner/best-age-to-for-kindergarten/

Cullins, A. (2022a, October 22). *Key strategies to teach children empathy (Sorted by Age).* Big Life Journal. https://biglifejournal.com/blogs/blog/key-strategies-teach-children-empathy

Cullins, A. (2022b, December 5). *7 ways to instill a love of learning in children.* Big Life Journal. https://biglifejournal.com/blogs/blog/instill-love-learning-children

Desai, A. (2020, June 5). *Home environment and its effect on a child's growth and development with relevant case laws.* Linkedin.

https://www.linkedin.com/pulse/home-environment-its-effect-childs-growth-development-s-desai/

Drew, C. (2019, December 13). *Peer to peer learning - Examples, pros & cons.* Helpful Professor. https://helpfulprofessor.com/peer-learning/

Gowmon, V. (2019, May 29). *Inspiring quotes on child learning and development - Vince Gowmon.* Vince Gowmon. https://www.vincegowmon.com/inspiring-quotes-on-child-learning-and-development/

Gupta, S. (2023, January 6). *Importance of value education: Aim, types, purpose, methods.* CollegeSearch. https://www.collegesearch.in/articles/importance-of-value-education#:~:text=Value%2Dbased%20education%20places%20an

Herzing Blog. (2022, February 4). *Top 7 myths about early childhood education, training, and careers.* Blog.herzing.ca. https://blog.herzing.ca/top-myths-about-early-childhood-education-training-career

Hoffses, K. (2018). *10 ways to help your child succeed in elementary school (for Parents).* Kidshealth. https://kidshealth.org/en/parents/school-help-elementary.html

Howard, L. (2020, April 29). *Why is empathy important for kids? Tips to build empathy in children.* Atlanta Innovative Counseling Center.

https://www.atlantainnovativecounseling.com/
aicc-blog/why-is-empathy-important-for-kids-
tips-to-build-empathy-in-children

Li, P. (2018, March 30). *Teaching kids respect - 6 highly
effective tips.* Parenting for Brain.
https://www.parentingforbrain.com/6-
controversial-tips-teaching-kids-respect/

Li, P. (2022, October 21). *50 inspiring parenting quotes that
get you through hard times.* Parenting for Brain.
https://www.parentingforbrain.com/parenting-
quotes/

Lyness, D. (2018, July 1). *Your child's self-esteem (for Parents).*
KidsHealth.
https://kidshealth.org/en/parents/self-
esteem.html#:~:text=Self%2Desteem%20helps
%20kids%20cope

Mcilroy, T. (2021, April 29). *Why listening skills in early
childhood are vital + how to teach them.* Empowered
Parents.
https://empoweredparents.co/listening-skills-
in-early-childhood/

Miracle Recreation. (2019, December 17). *How to make
learning fun.* Miracle Recreation.
https://www.miracle-
recreation.com/blog/how-to-make-learning-
fun/?lang=can

Mohan, D. (2018, November 14). *Top 9 Ways To Teach
Your Child How To Be Respectful And Humble.*
ParentCircle.

https://www.parentcircle.com/teaching-
children-about-respect-and-humility/article

Morin, A. (2012, July 17). *Why it is important to discipline
your child.* Verywell Family.
https://www.verywellfamily.com/why-it-is-
important-to-discipline-your-child-1094790

Morin, A. (2021, April 1). *Teaching kids self-discipline so they
can grow up to reach their goals.* Verywell Family.
https://www.verywellfamily.com/teach-kids-
self-discipline-skills-1095034

Morin, A. (2022, November 2). *These parenting quotes will
help you keep things in perspective.* Verywell Family.
https://www.verywellfamily.com/inspirational-
parenting-quotes-1094736

Noreen, R., Majid, A., & Rana, K. (2019). Activity-Based
Teaching versus Traditional Method of Teaching
in Mathematics at Elementary Level. *Bulletin of
Education and Research, 41(2),* 145-159.

Paul, M. (2022, February 2). *10 life skills for kids they must
learn before kindergarten.* Orchids.
https://www.orchidsinternationalschool.com/b
log/social-skills/life-skills-for-kids/

Saha, M. K. (2015, January 18). *"Tell me and I forget, teach
me and I may remember, involve me and I learn."-
Benjamin Franklin.* Linkedin.
https://www.linkedin.com/pulse/tell-me-i-

forget-teach-may-remember-involve-learn-
benjamin-saha/

Simpson, A. (2021, October 25). *How to use technology in
the early elementary classroom.* Nearpod Blog.
https://nearpod.com/blog/how-to-use-
technology-in-the-early-elementary-classroom/

Sitwell, S. (2021, December 3). *PBL in the early elementary
grades.*   Edutopia.
https://www.edutopia.org/article/pbl-early-
elementary-grades/

Weller, C. (2017, March 20). *Parents may be sending kids to
school too early in life, according to Stanford researchers.*
Business   Insider.
https://www.businessinsider.in/tech/parents-
may-be-sending-kids-to-school-too-early-in-life-
according-to-stanford-
researchers/articleshow/57738593.cms#:~:text
=Now%2C%20new%20research%20finds%20t
hey

Made in the USA
Middletown, DE
29 August 2024

59991953R00075